William Forbes Skene, Gustav Bickell

The Lord's Supper and the Passover Ritual

A Translation

William Forbes Skene, Gustav Bickell

The Lord's Supper and the Passover Ritual
A Translation

ISBN/EAN: 9783337336745

Printed in Europe, USA, Canada, Australia, Japan

Cover: Foto ©Lupo / pixelio.de

More available books at **www.hansebooks.com**

The Lord's Supper

and

The Passover Ritual;

BEING A

TRANSLATION OF THE SUBSTANCE OF PROFESSOR BICKELL'S WORK
TERMED "MESSE UND PASCHA."

By WILLIAM F. SKENE, D.C.L.

WITH AN INTRODUCTION BY THE TRANSLATOR

ON THE

Connection of the Early Christian Church with the Jewish Church.

EDINBURGH:
T. & T. CLARK, 38 GEORGE STREET.
1891.

TABLE OF CONTENTS.

	PAGE
TRANSLATOR'S PREFACE,	vii
TRANSLATOR'S INTRODUCTION,	1
AUTHOR'S PREFACE,	64
AUTHOR'S INTRODUCTION,	66

I.

THE PRIMITIVE CHRISTIAN LITURGY.

§ 1. The Liturgy of the Apostolical Constitutions,	70
§ 2. The other Liturgies,	78
§ 3. Superior Antiquity of the Clementine Liturgy,	86
§ 4. Use of the Clementine Liturgy during the first three Centuries,	101

II.

THE JEWISH RITUAL WHICH GAVE RISE TO THE OLD CHRISTIAN LITURGY.

§ 1. The Ritual of the Passover Supper,	111
§ 2. Antiquity of the Jewish Passover Ritual,	129
§ 3. The Sabbath-Morning Prayer,	141

III.

COMPARISON OF THE APOSTOLIC LITURGY WITH THE CORRESPONDING JEWISH RITUAL.

	PAGE
§ 1. The Institution of the Holy Eucharist in its connection with the Passover Supper,	159
§ 2. The Ante-Communion,	174
§ 3. The Canon or Anaphora,	195
§ 4. Dogmatic Conclusions,	215

TRANSLATOR'S PREFACE.

THE English and the German schools of liturgical writers present in some respects a marked contrast to each other. Notwithstanding the various learned works which have been written by English liturgical scholars, it cannot be said with any truth that the ancient Liturgies have been as yet subjected by them to a sufficiently thorough and comprehensive analysis; and in this respect the German scholars show a marked superiority. Unfortunately, till recently, English liturgical writers have in the main belonged to one school of thought in the Church, and have approached the subject with prepossessions and assumptions which have coloured the medium through which they have viewed the subject. On the other hand, the German liturgical scholars are in the main free from any bias of this kind, and exhibit more of that independent, accurate, and comprehensive research, and of that power of discriminating justly between what is based upon trustworthy authority and what rests upon questionable tradition without fear of results, which so eminently characterises the German mind.

The leading authority among English writers is unquestionably the Reverend William Palmer, who prefixes to his well-known *Origines Liturgicæ* a dissertation on primitive Liturgies; and he may justly be considered as the founder of the English school of Liturgiologists, as his conclusions have been adopted as certain truths by all subsequent writers; but when we examine the grounds on which many of them rest, they do not stand the test of critical examination. The general ground on which his system is based he thus states: "The following is the course which I have pursued in endeavouring to ascertain the nature of the primitive Liturgies. Considering that the primitive Church was divided into great portions, known by the appellations of Patriarchates, Enarchates, or national Churches, and that the supreme bishops in these districts (where there were such bishops) had generally sufficient influence in later ages to cause their Liturgies to be universally received by their suffragans, I thought it advisable, in the first place, to examine the Liturgies of such supreme Churches, and inquire whether they appear to be derived from primitive antiquity." The result of this mode of viewing the subject is that he reduces the primitive Liturgies to four — the great Oriental Liturgy, the Alexandrian, the Roman, and the Gallican; and these four great Liturgies, he says, appear to have been the parents of all the forms now extant. The fallacy of this system is that Liturgies are undoubtedly more ancient than Patriarchates, and existed in the Churches before that process of centralisation erected them into these great districts; and while, it is true, that one form of Liturgy in the main prevailed in each Patriarchate, yet before this bond of union existed there is every reason to suppose that a greater diversity of Liturgies prevailed in the Church till they were superseded by one general form. In the second century, and even in the third, every town of any consideration had certainly its own service as much as its own constitution, and used therefore its liturgic liberty.[1] Palmer's theory thus leads to his assigning a greater antiquity to the form of Liturgy that afterwards prevailed, and to crediting it with the same weight in earlier times that it afterwards possessed. Thus finding that the Church of Jerusalem possessed a Liturgy which passed under the name of St. James the first Bishop of Jerusalem, and that the Bishop of this Church became the Patriarch of the later Patriarchate, he assumes that though only mentioned for the first time in the sixth century, it must be held to be the parent of all the forms used in the Patriarchate, and gives it a prominence and an importance which is based upon mere assumption, and not upon historical authority. This assumption, however, leads him into a difficulty, for there is

---

[1] Bunsen, *Analecta Anteniceœna*, viii. p. 20.

another ancient Liturgy which differs from that of St. James, and has every claim to greater antiquity. That is the Liturgy preserved in the eighth book of the *Apostolical Constitutions,* and usually called the Clementine. Mr. Palmer admits that it is certainly a monument of venerable antiquity, but he gets out of this difficulty by a view which is certainly antecedently very improbable. He says that he cannot think that is to be considered as an accurate transcript of the Liturgy of any Church; that there is no evidence that it was used anywhere, and that it is the work of some unknown author, who affixed to it the name of Clement of Rome, and " has permitted his learning and devotion to enrich the common formularies with numerous ideas full of piety and beauty."

Another difficulty, too, was created by his theory, which imposed upon him the necessity of finding a parent Liturgy for each Patriarchate differing from those of the others. He was unable to point to any of the ancient Liturgies which he could assign, in his mode of viewing the subject, to the Patriarchate of Ephesus, and this difficulty he solved by assuming that it is represented by the Gallican Liturgy, which by an ingenious theory he endeavoured to show was derived from it; but these two hypotheses, though they are evidently based upon mere conjecture, to which Mr. Palmer's ingenuity has given a plausible appearance, have yet been adopted by all subsequent writers of this school as if they were undoubted facts.

The first and most thorough of the German writers on the Liturgies was Drey in his *Neue Untersuchungen*, but he dealt mainly with the Clementine Liturgy. In 1864 appeared an elaborate work by Hoppe on the Epiklesis of the Greek and Oriental Liturgies; but Dr. Ferdinand Probst, professor of Theology in the University of Breslau, may be regarded as the founder of the German liturgical school in his work on the Liturgies of the first three Christian centuries (*Liturgie der drei ersten Christlichen Jahrhunderte*), which contains an elaborate analysis of the ancient Liturgies. In this work he repudiates altogether Mr. Palmer's theory of the character of the Clementine Liturgy, and demonstrates that it was the oldest form of the liturgical service, and was in use in the Church of Antioch till it was superseded by the Liturgy of St. Basil. He was followed shortly after by Professor Bickell in his work, *The Lord's Supper and the Passover* (*Messe und Pascha*), who laid down the proposition that any Liturgy framed in apostolic times must have been derived to a great extent in its form and expression from the Synagogue service of the Jews and the ritual of the Passover Supper, in both of which the apostles had taken part; and shows that of all the ancient Liturgies the Clementine is the one which approaches most nearly, and shows the greatest correspondence with, the Jewish forms, and has the greatest claim to be considered the apostolic Liturgy from which all others have been derived.

These two important works have not been translated, and the object of this work is to bring the substance of them under the notice of English writers by a translation of nearly the whole of Professor Bickell's work, to which is prefixed an Introduction by the translator on the relations between the early Christian and the Jewish Churches.

W. F. S.

TRANSLATOR'S INTRODUCTION.

THE history of the Christian Church during the apostolic time falls naturally into distinct periods, which were characterised by peculiar influences that affected her, and in consequence gave rise to peculiar features in her constitution and development. An indication of these periods is afforded to us in the address which our Saviour gave to the apostles in the opening chapter of the Acts, when He said, "*But ye shall receive power when the Holy Ghost is come upon you; and ye shall be my witnesses both in Jerusalem, and in all Judea, and Samaria, and unto the uttermost parts of the earth.*" We have thus, first, the period when the Church was confined to Jerusalem; secondly, when it spread throughout all Judea and Samaria; and thirdly, when it extended to the Gentiles. The close of the first period is marked by the persecution which followed the martyrdom of St. Stephen, when "*there was a great persecution against the Church which was at Jerusalem; and they were all scattered abroad throughout the regions of Judea and Samaria, except the apostles*" (chap. viii. 1). The close of the second, when Paul and Barnabas were separated for the work whereunto they were called, and were sent forth by the Holy Ghost; and when, after preaching to the Jews in the synagogue at Antioch in Pisidia, they said to them, "*It was necessary that the word of God should first have been spoken to you; but seeing ye put it from you, and judge yourselves unworthy of everlasting life, lo, we turn to the Gentiles.*" "*And when the Gentiles heard this they were glad, and glorified the word of the Lord; and as many as were ordained to eternal life believed.*" This took place in the year 45 of the Christian era. The Church was therefore, during the first fifteen years after the apostles received the Holy Ghost at Pentecost, a Jewish-Christian Church, and its members consisted of the two classes of Jews, those called Hebrews, who spoke Aramaic, and those called Hellenists, who spoke Greek. After this date, while the Church at Jerusalem remained Jewish till the fall of Jerusalem, the Church elsewhere was in the main a Gentile-Christian Church. In towns where there was a mixed population of Jews and Greeks, and where many of the former had received the faith, the Church founded among them may have consisted of both; but in the great cities of Europe the Church was in the main a purely Gentile Church.

When the Church was thus introduced among the Gentiles it must, to some extent at least, have come with a fixed constitution and ritual; but, as in the

Jewish-Christian Church the members had emerged from the Jewish Church of the old dispensation and were familiar with its rites and ceremonies, it is impossible to estimate rightly the character of the Church in its earliest stage, and of its constitution and ritual, without inquiring to what extent its original organisation may have been influenced by Jewish forms and ideas.

In making this inquiry it will, however, be necessary, as an indispensable preliminary, to discriminate between the different forms of worship in the old dispensation, as well as between the different parties associated with each. Before the Babylonian captivity the only stated worship among the Jews was that, first, of the tabernacle, and afterwards of the temple at Jerusalem. It consisted of the regular morning and evening sacrifice, of the special sacrifices and offerings prescribed by the law, and the three great annual festivals of the Passover, Pentecost, or the Feast of Weeks, and the Feast of Tabernacles, to which every male Jew was bound to come. To the temple worship the functions of the priests and Levites were entirely confined. Although it is plain from the narratives of the New Testament that there were in our Saviour's days synagogues in every town and city, and even in the larger villages throughout, not only Judea, but also in Samaria and Galilee, and that a form of worship in the synagogue prevailed everywhere, the synagogue service was not in any way connected with or formed part of the temple worship. Its origin, in fact, was much more recent. Before the captivity we find no trace of synagogues in the Old Testament; but during the captivity in Babylon, when the temple worship had necessarily ceased, it became customary for the more devout Jews to pray privately in an upper room, having a window looking towards Jerusalem, which they opened during prayer.

After the Jews returned from the captivity, and Jerusalem was rebuilt, it became necessary to promulgate anew the laws of Moses, and to make the people generally acquainted with them. In order to effect this, the people were assembled everywhere on the Sabbath to hear the law read to them and expounded. We read in the Book of Nehemiah, chap. viii., that the people were gathered together to hear the law of Moses, which was read before the congregation, both of men and women, and all that could hear with understanding, from a pulpit of wood, by Ezra and other doctors from morning till mid-day, having first "*blessed the Lord, the great God; and all the people answered, Amen.*" Here the word congregation is equivalent to synagogue; and here we have the outline of the synagogue service, which consisted of praise and thanksgiving, the people answering, Amen, the Book of the Law being read from a pulpit of wood, followed by explanation.

The synagogues were soon multiplied through the land, and it became an established rule that a synagogue was erected in every town or village of at least 120 inhabitants, where there were ten men of leisure, of full age and free condition, who could undertake to attend all the synagogue services and take part in them. The result of the establishment of the synagogue worship, which brought the teaching of the Law home to every town and village in the land, was that, while under the temple worship, which was confined to Jerusalem, the Jews were constantly relapsing into idolatry, which led at last to their captivity, after their return to their own land they adhered stedfastly to the worship of the one true God.

About the same time that the synagogue worship was established, the confraternity of the *sopherim* or scribes makes its appearance, and was closely connected with the synagogues. As the latter was primarily designed as a means for instructing the Jewish people in the law, and influencing them to a strict observance of it, so the scribes were the teachers and expounders of the law, and as such they are termed in the New Testament, also lawyers (νομικοί) and teachers of the law (νομοδιδάσκαλοι). They had their schools in the synagogue, in which the Jewish children, as soon as they reached the age of twelve, were instructed in the law, and they taught in the synagogues during the stated service. In enforcing the strict observance of the law in the minutest particular, they created by degrees an unwritten code, in which its sanctions were overlaid by a number of minute observances to every detail of social life, which rendered it burdensome to the last degree.

Of the two great religious parties into which the Jewish nation was divided, viz. the Sadducees and the Pharisees, the priests and those connected with the temple worship belonged, at our Saviour's time, to the sect of the Sadducees, but the scribes and doctors of the law to the sect of the Pharisees. The scribes and the Pharisees were thus the learned and constitutional party among the Jews, who framed their conduct according to the rules of that traditionary and oral law of which they were the bigoted adherents. Their sphere was the synagogue, and their business the teaching of the law and enforcing its precepts. The Sadducees were not adherents of this unwritten law. They would not consider any offence against it as subjecting the offender to a penalty. They looked only to the temporal prosperity of the nation, and were actuated by motives of policy and expediency. Their sphere was the temple, and their business its sacrificial worship.

Our Saviour, during His ministry on earth, fulfilled the obligation imposed by the law upon every male among the children of Israel to attend the three great temple feasts at Jerusalem; but as, in practice, this obligation was limited to persons residing within fifteen miles of the city, while those at a greater distance were only expected to attend one of the feasts, Jesus, as a native of Galilee, seems only to have attended one of the three great feasts in each year of His ministry.

That ministry was opened at the Passover feast when He commenced His public teaching. In the second year he went to the Feast of Weeks or Pentecost.[1] In the third year He attended the Feast of Tabernacles, and in the winter the Feast of Dedication; while He concluded His ministry by attending a second time the Feast of the Passover, when He went to Jerusalem to be delivered up to the Jews and crucified.

On these occasions He taught in the temple, but His opponents were the scribes and Pharisees. He had early come in contact with these doctors of the law. He was found at the age of twelve, when taken to the temple to be presented, sitting among the doctors disputing with them, and asking and answering questions as their scholars were wont to do. At His appearance at the temple in the first year of His ministry, when He openly announced Himself as the long-expected Messiah, the scribes and Pharisees do not seem to have been indisposed to recognise, on account of the miracles which accompanied His teaching, and which were in accordance with them, that the Old Testament prophets

---

[1] This is the feast which St. John refers to in his Gospel as "a feast of the Jews," without naming it. It has been supposed by some to be the Passover, and by others the Feast of Tabernacles; but as St. John mentions these by name, it is not likely that he could have meant either by this feast. The idea entertained by some that it was the Feast of Purim, a subordinate feast instituted to commemorate the relief afforded to the Jews by Esther, is utterly incredible; but the connection of the events immediately before and after points to the Feast of Weeks or Pentecost, and this is in accordance with the early traditions of the Church.

had foretold would be a characteristic of the Messiah; but at the Feast of Pentecost, when He incurred the resentment of the scribes and Pharisees by His refusal to recognise the restrictions they had imposed upon the observance of the Sabbath, and openly announced Himself as the Son of God and as real Lord of the Sabbath, "the Pharisees went out, and held council against Him, how they might destroy Him." They would not have considered that the claim Jesus made to be their Messiah involved any crime, even if they did not accept it. That was a question with regard to which they would examine the evidence on which it rested, and either confirm or deny His claim. Neither did the declaration that the judgment of the world had been committed to Him by God involve anything they need take hold of, for they believed in a future state, in which the good would be rewarded and the wicked punished, and admitted that the Messiah would execute that judgment; but they could not forgive His open disregard of their laws for keeping the Sabbath holy, and considered that His having done so presumptuously subjected Him to the penalty of death by stoning. On the other hand, the Sadducees did not accept the unwritten law of the scribes and Pharisees, and disbelieved in a future state; but both parties agreed in the opinion that the Messiah would be a mere man, and viewed with horror any view that appeared to conflict with the unity of God, and therefore the declaration by Jesus of His essential divinity as the Son of God appeared to them to involve the far greater crime of blasphemy, and on this ground they rejected Him, and resolved to effect His destruction. Thus St. John tells us, "*Therefore, the Jews sought the more to kill Him, not only because He had broken the Sabbath, but said also that God was His Father, making Himself equal with God.*"

Jesus having been thus rejected by the scribes and Pharisees, now turned to another class of the community which had peculiar claims upon His sympathy. Among the Jews, their nation was distinguished into two great classes. These were the "scholars," or "disciples of the wise," and "the people of the land." The first class was composed of those who had been trained in the study of the law, and to this class belonged the scribes and Pharisees. The other class comprised the unlearned, or those who knew not the law. They were, in fact, the common people, and were looked upon with great contempt by the Pharisees, and had no instruction whatever afforded them. Thus we find the Pharisees saying, "*But this people, who knoweth not the law, are cursed*" (John vii. 49); and in the books of the Jews we find the same contempt expressed for them. Their neglected state appealed largely to the compassion of Jesus. Thus St. Matthew tells us that when Jesus "*saw the multitudes, He was moved with compassion on them, because they fainted, and were scattered abroad as sheep having no shepherd*" (ix. 36). He was probably the first Teacher who had ever addressed any instruction to them, and He refers to them when He says, "*I am not sent but unto the lost sheep of the house of Israel*" (Matt. xv. 34). These people had now been roused out of their sluggish condition, first by the preaching of John the Baptist, and afterwards by the fame of the miracles done by Jesus, and the startling novelty of His teaching, which gave them hopes that they, too, might be admitted into the kingdom of God which was at hand. They now flocked after Him wherever they heard that this new Prophet was to be met, and, as St. Mark tells us, "*the common people heard Him gladly*" (xii. 37). On His return to Galilee they now came to Him from Judea, or the land north of Jerusalem, where He had healed the man with the withered hand, and proclaimed Himself Lord of the Sabbath. They came to Him from Jerusalem, where He had healed the impotent man at the Pool of Bethesda in the presence of the people. They came to Him from Idumea, as the southern part of Judea was then called; and from beyond Jordan, when He went along the east bank of the river towards Galilee; and they assembled around Him when He reached the Sea of Galilee. Here He first relieved them from their physical evils by healing the sick and casting out unclean spirits, from whom He received that recognition which had been withheld from Him by the Pharisees, for, "*when they saw Him, they fell down before Him, and cried out, saying, Thou art the Son of God*" (Mark iii. 11); and then addressed to them that great discourse, the Sermon on the Mount.

While Jesus thus, on the single occasions when He visited Jerusalem for one of the great feasts, addressed Himself to the cultivated classes among the Jews who frequented the synagogue, to the Pharisees and scribes or doctors of the law, He still continued, when He was not addressing the people in the open-air, to teach in the synagogues, proving from the books of the prophets that He was the promised Messiah. The evangelists repeatedly mention that it was His wont. Thus St. Matthew tells us, that "*Jesus went about all the cities and villages, teaching in their synagogues and preaching the gospel of the kingdom*" (iv. 23). St. Luke, that "*He taught in their synagogues, being glorified of all,*" and that "*He preached in the synagogue of Galilee*" (iv. 15, 44); and in His trial before the high priest, Jesus says, "*I spake openly to the world; I ever taught in the synagogue, and in the temple, whither the Jews always resort; and in secret have I said nothing*" (St. John xviii. 20); but during this time "*the scribes and Pharisees watched Him, that they might find accusation against Him.*"

At length when Jesus went to Jerusalem, in the second year of His ministry, to the Feast of Tabernacles, the crisis came which led to His forming His disciples into a community separate from the Jewish worship, which He termed His Church. Here He again encountered the scribes and Pharisees in the temple, and plainly and emphatically declared that He came from God, and His pre-existence as the Son of God before

He came upon the earth. The scribes and Pharisees, who had on His previous visit gone about to kill Him, now seeing how He was winning the people, took the decided step of deciding "*that if any man did confess that He was Christ, he should be put out of the synagogue.*" This was the Jewish sentence of excommunication, and should be inflicted, not simply because they recognised Jesus as the Messiah, but because such recognition involved that of accepting Him as the Son of God. It was a serious penalty, for it cut off the sufferer from the nation of Israel, separated him from all social intercourse with the Jewish people, and debarred him from the worship of the synagogue, though not from access to the temple. This at once placed the followers of Jesus in a position of entire separation from the nation of which they hitherto formed a part, through recognising Him as the Messiah, and from all the privileges attached to it; and from this time it was unavoidable that they should form a separate community. The first victim under this decree was the man, born blind, whose sight Jesus restored, and who, refusing to admit that Jesus, who had restored to sight one born blind, could have done so unless He possessed divine power, was cast out of the synagogue; and to Him Jesus revealed Himself personally as the Son of God, and he worshipped Him. The next event, and one in direct connection with this, was that Jesus, having gone from Jerusalem to the coasts of Cæsarea Philippi, asked His disciples, "*Whom say ye that I* am? and Simon Peter answered, *Thou art Christ, the Son of the living God.*" And He then said, "*Upon this rock I will build my Church.*" Upon this confession, that Jesus was the Christ or Messiah, declaring Himself to be the Son of God, any one making it was excommunicated by the Jews. On this confession by Simon Peter that He was Christ, the Son of the living God, He would build His Church as a separate community. The Church is built upon its creeds; and this was the first creed of the Christian Church, that Jesus was the Christ, the Son of the living God. But it was necessary that this truth should be clearly recognised by His other disciples; and therefore He carried out the purpose for which He, no doubt, had come to Cæsarea Philippi, that of going to a high mountain and showing them what His essential glory was when He was transfigured before three of their number, as selected witnesses of it, when God's glory overshadowed them in a bright cloud, and a voice from heaven declared, "*This is my beloved Son; hear ye Him.*"

Thus, as when Jesus begun His public mission to the Jews as their Messiah by His baptism, a voice from heaven proclaimed the divine character of His mission, "*This is my beloved Son, in whom I am well pleased;*" so the first announcement of the Christian Church which He was to found was inaugurated by a similar proclamation from heaven.

The Christian Church was thus to come in place of the synagogue; and the privileges conferred upon St.

Peter, and afterwards upon all the disciples, were those which belonged to the scribes. They were the authorised interpreters of the oral and traditionary laws which had been superinduced upon the law of Moses; and in this capacity they were held by the Jews to possess the key of the kingdom of heaven. Thus when Jesus denounced them for their abuse of this power, He said, according to St. Matthew, "*Woe unto you, scribes and Pharisees, hypocrites! for ye shut up the kingdom of heaven against men: for ye neither go in yourselves, neither suffer ye them that are entering to go in*" (xxiii. 13); and in the parallel passage in St. Luke it is, "*Woe unto you, lawyers! for ye have taken away the key of knowledge: ye enter not in yourselves, and them that were entering in ye hindered.*"

The power thus exercised by the scribes was known to the Jews as that of binding and loosing. This was a power which refers to things, not to persons, and was one of the privileges claimed by the scribes or Rabbis. It was the mode by which they expressed their decision as to what was prohibited and what was permitted by the traditionary law of the elders.[2] These powers are now conferred upon St. Peter: "*I will give unto thee the keys of the kingdom of heaven: and whatsoever thou shalt bind on earth shall be bound in heaven; and whatsoever thou shalt loose on earth shall be loosed in heaven.*"

---

[2] The expression occurs in this sense constantly in the Talmud, and mainly in the controversies between the two great schools of the scribes with those of Schammai and of Hillel.

The same power of binding and loosing was extended to all the apostles after the transfiguration, which appears to have brought the same conviction to them as to St. Peter. On this occasion, too, we find the Church taking the place of the synagogue. By the term brother the Jews understood an Israelite by nation and religion, in contrast with a proselyte and a heathen; and a practice was founded upon the injunction in the Book of Leviticus (xix. 17), "*Thou shalt not hate thy brother in thine heart: thou shalt in any wise rebuke thy neighbour, and not suffer sin upon him.*" Their rule was that any one against whom a sin had been committed must "deliver his soul by reproving his brother;" and if he could not bring him back to the right way, he must reprove him before witnesses, so that they might testify that he against whom the sin was committed used due reproof, the witnesses also adding their friendly admonition; and if the offender hearkened not unto them, then they made proclamation concerning him in the synagogues for four Sabbaths. Jesus here directs the same procedure to be adopted, only substituting the church for the synagogue: "*If thy brother sin against thee, go and tell him his fault between thee and him alone: if he shall hear thee, thou hast gained thy brother. But if he will not hear thee, then take with thee one or two more, that in the mouth of two or three witnesses every word may be established. And if he shall neglect to hear them, tell it unto the Church.*" Again, by the custom of the Jews there could be no synagogue unless there were ten men of leisure who could attend its services regularly; and it came to be a belief among them, that unless these ten men were present their prayers in the synagogue were not heard by God. But Jesus vindicates the efficacy of common prayer without any condition as to numbers; for He said that if even "*two of you shall agree on earth as touching anything that they shall ask, it shall be done for them of my Father which is in heaven. For where two or three are gathered together in my name, there am I in the midst of them.*"

Having thus indicated the character of His Church which was to replace the synagogue worship, Jesus now impresses upon His disciples three great moral qualities which should characterise them in their conduct of it at all times. These were humility, toleration, and love. Humility, for, "*Verily I say unto you, Except ye be converted, and become as little children, ye shall not enter the kingdom of heaven. Whosoever therefore shall humble himself as this little child, the same is greatest in the kindgom of heaven.*" Toleration, when St. John says to Him, "*Master, we saw one casting out devils in Thy name, and he followeth not us; and we forbade him, because he followeth not us. But Jesus said, Forbid him not: for there is no man which shall do a miracle in my name, that can speak evil of me. For he that is not against us is on our part.*" That is, that they ought not to look solely to external communion with them, but also to the internal relation to Himself, and if they are advancing His cause. Love, when St. Peter says to Him,

"*Lord, how oft shall my brother sin against me, and I forgive him? till seven times?*" In saying this he no doubt thought he was showing a spirit of great charity towards his brother, for the rule of the Jews was that forgiveness was only required three times; but Jesus answered, "*I say not unto thee, Till seven times; but, Until seventy times seven;*" that is, he must put no limit to the exercise of love towards a brother.

Jesus having thus laid the foundation of His Church and fulfilled His mission in Galilee, which led to a large number of its population accepting Him as their Messiah, was now to leave Galilee finally for Jerusalem, where He was to accomplish His passion; but He was still to make another great step in advance in the organisation of His Church. St. Matthew tells us that "*When Jesus had finished these sayings,*"—viz. those containing His great lessons of humility, toleration, and love,—"*He departed from Galilee, and came into the coasts of Judea beyond Jordan: and great multitudes followed Him.*" But St. Luke states more precisely the object of His journey; he says, "*When the time was come that He should be received up, He stedfastly set His face to go to Jerusalem, and sent messengers before His face: and they went and entered into a village of the Samaritans, to make ready for Him. And they did not receive Him, because His face was as though He would go to Jerusalem.*" Jesus then altered His route, and did not pass through Samaria. But St. Luke tells us that "*After these things He appointed other seventy also, and sent them two and two before His face, into every city and place whither He Himself would come."* This was a mission similar to that on which He had formerly sent the apostles two and two to preach that kingdom of God, for the instructions given to the seventy were very similar. They were sent as labourers into the harvest. They had power to heal the sick, and were to say unto them, "*The kingdom of God is come nigh unto you;*" and Jesus concluded His instructions by saying, "*He that heareth you, heareth me; and he that despiseth you, despiseth me; and he that despiseth me, despiseth Him that sent me;*" or as in the Revised Version, "*He that rejecteth you rejecteth me; and he that rejecteth me rejecteth Him that sent me.*" This was therefore a body of missionaries similar in position and functions to that of the twelve apostles, to aid them in view of the future extension of the Christian Church. In this respect they resembled the seventy elders whom God directed Moses to bring into the tabernacle of the congregation, that they might stand there with him. "*And the Lord came down in a cloud, and spake unto him, and took of the spirit that was upon Him, and gave it to the seventy elders; and it came to pass when the spirit rested upon them, they prophesied, and did not cease.*"

It is hardly possible to avoid the conclusion that it was in reference to this body that the number of the additional missionaries was fixed at seventy, and that they were to occupy the same position towards the apostles in the new dispensation which the seventy elders did towards Moses in the old; and that, like them, when the Holy Spirit would rest upon them at the day of Pentecost, they too, as well as all who received, would have the gift of prophecy, and would become known by the name of prophets.

There were thus now two orders established in the future Christian Church, viz. the apostles and the seventy; and this is very clearly indicated when, according to St. Matthew, Jesus says at a later period to the scribes and Pharisees, "*Wherefore, behold, I send unto you prophets, and wise men, and scribes: and some of them ye shall kill and crucify; and some of them shall ye scourge in your synagogues, and persecute them from city to city*" (xxiii. 34); but in the parallel passage in St. Luke's Gospel it is, "*Therefore also said the wisdom of God, I will send them prophets and apostles: and some of them they shall slay and persecute.*" In these passages the prophets are named first, for the apostles possessed the gift of prophecy, and were in a sense included in the designation; but St. Luke clearly identifies the apostles as being the persons meant by the term wise men and scribes, whose functions had been so distinctly transferred to them. Both the apostles and the seventy were appointed by Jesus Himself, and both were to be qualified for their ministry by the gift of the Holy Spirit.

As far as we have gone the mission of the Christian Church was twofold. First, the ministerial work of supplying public worship to her children, and teaching in room of the synagogue ; and secondly, the missionary work of preaching the kingdom of God to those without ; but two very important features of the Church were to be added before the Saviour was received up into heaven. These were the Sacraments of Baptism and the Lord's Supper. The latter was first instituted in connection with the Jewish Passover, which our Saviour celebrated the evening before He was crucified, and which was destined to form the principal feature in the worship of the Christian Church. It will be more particularly adverted to afterwards in connection with the ritual of the Church. The former was instituted after our Saviour's resurrection and before His ascension, and was connected with the missionary character of the Church, just as it was connected with the missionary proceedings of the Jewish Church ; for when they made proselytes of the heathen, they received them into the Jewish Church, not by circumcision, but by baptism. The command was given to His disciples, "*Go, teach all nations, baptizing them in the name of the Father, and the Son, and the Holy Ghost.*" Finally, when Jesus met seven of the disciples at the Sea of Tiberias and gave St. Peter the injunction to feed His sheep, this term was applied by Him emphatically to the people of Israel, whom He designates as the lost sheep of the house of Israel; and it was, no doubt, over these sheep that Simon Peter was especially appointed shepherd. It is probably to this very passage that St. Paul alludes when he says, as it is more correctly rendered in the Revised Version, that he had been entrusted with the gospel of the uncircumcision, even as Peter with the gospel of the circumcision (Gal. ii. 8).

Such was the preparation which our Saviour made for the organisation of the Christian Church before the ascension to heaven. It was to come in place of the synagogue worship of the Jews, and His apostles were to be to the Christian Church what the scribes had been to the Jewish, and to possess similar privileges and exercise similar functions. Its teachers appear under the two designations of apostles and prophets. The former had a power of regulating for the Church; and in order to exercise these functions under divine influence they would be endowed with power from on high, when the Holy Spirit would descend upon them on the day of Pentecost; but before that event took place they had to complete their number by ordaining one in room of the apostate Judas. On the day of the ascension then, when they had seen their Saviour received up into heaven, what may be called the first meeting of the Christian Church took place. It was held in an upper room; but this was not the same upper room in which the Passover supper had been held, for the Greek words applied to the two rooms are different, and have a different meaning. The word applied to the room in which the last supper was held (ἀνώγεον) is applied to any room in one of the upper storeys; but the word used for this upper room (ὑπερίζον) indicated the highest room in the house.

In all the houses of the Rabbis there was a large upper room built on the roof, called in Hebrew Beth Midras, which was set apart for the meeting of their disciples; and as St. Luke tells us that the eleven apostles abode in it, it was probably such an upper room in the house of a Rabbi, and may have been that of Nicodemus, who, if not a Christian, was friendly to them. There they all continued with one accord in prayer with the women, and Mary the mother of Jesus, and with His brethren who were not apostles, but, owing to the appearance of Christ after His resurrection to James one of these brethren, had now been converted. St. Luke tells us that the number of the disciples present were about one hundred and twenty; and his object in naming this number was, no doubt, to show, as they had met for an important purpose, that according to the ideas of the Jews it was a lawful assembly; for they held that as Ezra's great synagogue consisted of one hundred and twenty elders, there could be no lawful council held in any city under that number.[3] Of these ninety-two must be elders; and it is plain here that the seventy disciples were present, who with the apostles would make up that number. The remainder would be, as in the case of the Jewish number, individuals belonging to the body.

The main object of the meeting was to complete the number of the twelve apostles by appointing one in

---

[3] "How many are requisite in a city that it might be capable of having a council in it? a hundred and twenty."

room of Judas; but as an apostle could be appointed by Christ alone, they had to take some means of ascertaining the Lord's will in regard to the selection, and for this purpose adopted the mode employed with a similar object by the Jews on the day of atonement, where Aaron, and after him the high priest for the time, is directed "*to take two goats, and present them before the Lord at the door of the tabernacle of the congregation. And Aaron shall cast lots upon the two goats; one lot for the Lord, and the other lot for the scapegoat. And Aaron shall bring the goat upon which the Lord's lot fell, and offer him for a sin-offering.*" In a similar manner the apostles selected two disciples whom they thought most fit for the purpose, and "*gave forth their lots: and the lot fell upon Matthias: and he was numbered with the eleven apostles.*" The mode in which lots were taken among the Jews was to place in a vessel tablets upon which the names were written, and shake it, and the name which first fell out was selected; and a similar process may have been observed here. But as this was the adoption of a quite exceptional process in order to meet an exceptional case, it must not be taken as affording any rule for the selection of Christian functionaries in future. It will be observed that in one place St. Peter uses the word "$\delta\iota\alpha\varkappa o\nu\iota\alpha$," or ministry, to express the functions of an apostle, and in another, ministry ($\delta\iota\alpha\varkappa o\nu\iota\alpha$) and apostleship. That is, the word $\delta\iota\alpha\varkappa o\nu\iota\alpha$ was used at this time for the ministry in general, and apostleship for the particular functions of an apostle; and we find the word so used in the New Testament till the order of deacons became established in the Gentile-Christian Church, when it is used in a more restricted sense.

In the last command which our Saviour gave the disciples just before the ascension, He desired them not to depart from Jerusalem, but wait for the promise of the Father, "*which ye have heard from me; for John truly baptized with water, but ye shall be baptized with the Holy Ghost not many days hence;*" and again, "*But ye shall receive power when the Holy Ghost is come upon you; and ye shall be my witnesses, both in Jerusalem and in all Judea and Samaria, and unto the uttermost parts of the earth;*" and now when "*the day of Pentecost was come, they were altogether in one place. And suddenly there came from heaven a sound, as of the rushing of a mighty wind, and it filled all the house where they were sitting. And there appeared unto them cloven tongues, as of fire, and it sat on each of them. And they were all filled with the Holy Ghost, and began to speak with other tongues, as the Spirit gave them utterance.*" These verses have been quoted at length, as it is necessary to advert to the precise meaning of some of the expressions. When it is said that "*they were all together,*" the word *all* seems to refer to the assembly held ten days before, on the day of ascension, and implies that the whole 120 disciples received the gift of the Holy Spirit. The expression one place is more properly the same place, that is, the upper room,[4] and the word "house," where they were sitting, confirms this. The effect produced by the outpouring of the Holy Spirit was twofold, as appears from St. Peter's statement, that this was a fulfilment of the prophecy of the prophet Joel compared with the subsequent notices of the effect of the Holy Spirit. It consisted, first, of the speaking with other tongues, as the Spirit gave them utterance; and secondly, prophesying; and hence the name of prophet was applied to those who had been directly under the influence of the Holy Spirit on that occasion. But this name, it must be recollected, was not only applied to those who foretold events, but also to those who were inspired preachers of righteousness, who have the mind of God and preach the word of God; and it is this prophesying that is meant when those who were present heard them speak in their tongues "the wonderful works of God." St. Peter then earnestly addressed the multitude, and the result was that *"they that gladly received his word were baptized: and there were added in that day about three thousand souls."*

This, then, was the actual formation of the Christian Church at Jerusalem; and we have a very valuable statement in few and significant words of the characteristics of this Church, when it is added, according to the Authorised Version, "*And they continued stedfast in*

---

[4] ἐπὶ τὸ αὐτό is repeatedly used at these meetings, and seems to imply a fixed place of meeting.

the apostles' doctrine and fellowship, and in breaking of bread and in prayers;" but this is not an accurate translation of the passage, and unfortunately this incorrect version has been retained in the Revised Version. The literal rendering of the passage is, "*And they continued stedfastly in the teaching of the apostles and in the communion, in the breaking of bread and in the prayers.*" There are thus four distinct features of the Church mentioned, and the mode in which they were practised is stated in the following verses. It is necessary here to attend to the Greek words used to express these four things. The word translated "teaching" is διδαχή. It is erroneously translated "doctrine" in the Authorised Version. The word used for doctrine throughout the New Testament is διδασκαλία; the term διδαχή is exclusively used in the sense of the realisation of the moral obligations and rules of the Christian life, and has no reference to dogmatic teaching. Thus it is applied by St. Matthew to the teaching of the Sermon on the Mount: "*The people were astonished at His doctrine,*" or, more correctly in the Revised Version, "*The multitudes were astonished at His teaching*" (διδαχή) (vii. 28). The Fathers of the Church used the word in the same sense. Thus St. Barnabas says, "Wherefore in one habitation God truly dwells in us. How? the word of faith, the calling of promise, this wisdom of statutes. His commands of διδαχή, He Himself prophesying to us;" and the context shows that these commands were moral (xvi. 9).

We have the two words contrasted in the following passage, which I take from the Revised Version: "*Holding fast to the faithful word which is according to the teaching* (διδαχή), *that he may be able both to exhort in the sound doctrine* (διδασκαλία), *and to convict the gainsayers*" (Tit. i. 9). St. Mark tells us that after the ascension, the apostles "*went forth and preached everywhere, the Lord working with them, and confirming the word by the signs which followed*" (xvi. 20); and here in reference to this teaching we are told, that "*fear, or rather awe, came upon every soul; and many wonders and signs were done by the apostles.*" The word translated "communion" is κοινωνία; and this word is used in the New Testament in two senses, first, as contributing to the support of the Church or of the poorer Christians, that is, giving of alms; and secondly, of fellowship. It occurs five times in the one sense and ten in the other. Thus St. Paul frequently uses it in the first sense as in Rom. xv. 26, "*For it hath pleased them of Macedonia and Achaia to make a certain contribution* (κοινωνία) *for the poor saints which are at Jerusalem;*" and likewise in the second sense as in 2 Cor. vi. 14, "*what fellowship* (κοινωνία) *hath light with darkness?*" Here the word is used in the former sense, and the precise mode in which it was practised is explained in the following verses: "*And all that believed were together, and had all things in common; and sold their possessions and goods, and parted them to all men, as every man had need.*"

This form of communion was forced upon them by the excommunication of the Jewish Christians from the synagogue, which had social consequences that cut off from the poorer members their means of earning a livelihood; and thus those who had means had to support their poorer brethren. So far as it may be termed a community of goods, it was peculiar to the Jewish-Christian Church, and not an essential feature of the Church in general.[5] One form of this communion was no doubt the common meal, afterwards termed the agape, which preceded the Lord's Supper. This is here termed "breaking of bread;" and the explanation is given, "*that they continued daily with one accord in the temple, and breaking bread from house to house,*" or more properly, at home, "*did eat their meat with gladness and singleness of heart, praising God, and having favour with all the people.*" We thus see that though excluded from the synagogues the temple was open to them; and of these four things, part took place daily in the temple and part at home. As we learn from other notices, the apostles taught there, and the people still resorted to it at the time of prayer; but the common meal, which is alluded to in the expression "*did eat their meat with gladness and singleness of heart,*" as well as the distribution of alms and the celebration of the Lord's Supper, which is meant by the expression of

---

[5] Something similar took place in India when the converted Hindu forfeited her caste and lost her means of livelihood, and the converts had to be taken into the mission station and supported.

breaking of bread, took place at home, that is, in the upper chamber where they met, and at the houses of the converts.

The effect of the preaching of the apostles in the temple, accompanied by signs and wonders, was soon apparent; for we are told that St. Peter and St. John, having gone to the temple and healed a man lame from his birth, and St. Peter having followed it with an address to the people, the result was that the number of believers was increased from 3000 to 5000 people. Of this number a considerable part must now have consisted of Hellenist Jews—St. Luke appears to indicate two parties; and when it is again said that the multitude of them that believed had all things in common (iv. 32), and (ver. 34) "*Neither was there any among them that lacked: for as many as were possessed of lands and houses sold them, and brought the prices of the things that were sold, and laid them down at the apostles' feet.*" Those who had all things in common were the Jews of Jerusalem, and with them the contribution of their entire possessions was, of course, compulsory; but these resources were supplemented by others who voluntarily sold lands or houses; and that these were the Hellenist Jews appears from the instances given, viz. Barnabas, a Hellenist Jew from Cyprus, and Ananias, whose contribution is expressly said to be voluntary. There was this difference between the two parties, that the Jews of Jerusalem, whose means of subsistence were cut off by their excommunication, were absolutely dependent upon the community of goods for their support; but the Hellenist Jews, who were not so closely connected with Jerusalem, had still the means of supporting themselves, and, while willing to add to the goods in communion, made no claim to share in them for their support. The only case in which such a claim could legitimately be made was in the case of widows who had been left destitute; and this claim led to an important change in the organisation of the Christian (διακονία or) ministry, by which its missionary and ministerial functions were separated, and a permanent provision made for the latter.

Hitherto these two functions had been united in the apostles; and we are told in chap. v. 42 that daily in the temple, and even in every house or at home, they ceased not to teach and preach Jesus Christ. They taught (διδάσκοντες) in the houses where the believers assembled, that is, their ministerial work; and they preached (εὐαγγελιζόμενοι) in the temple to the Jews, their missionary work. St. Luke now tells us that "*When the number of the disciples were multiplied,*" mainly by the addition of Hellenist Jews, "*there arose a murmuring of the Grecians,*" that is, the Hellenist Jews, "*against the Hebrews,*" or Jews of Jerusalem, "*because their widows were neglected in the daily ministration*" (διακονία). Then the apostles call together the multitude, or rather company, of the disciples, and represent to them that it is not meet that they should leave the word of God, and serve tables (διακονεῖν τραπέζαις). We have here again the distinction between the missionary and ministerial work of the Church, and the apostles propose now to separate them by confining themselves to prayer and to the ministry of the word (διακονία λογόυ), that is, to the work done in the temple of winning souls to Christ by preaching the gospel, and to ordain a permanent ministry for the ministerial work done at home, viz. the κοινωνία and the breaking of bread of the Eucharist, which were inseparably connected. The administration of charity and the worship of the synagogue were similarly connected among the Jews. There were in every city seven elders or presbyters, who were termed the seven good men of the city. They were ordained by the imposition of hands, and consisted of three men who were rulers of the synagogue, and performed its judicial functions; three *parnasim*, two to collect alms, and one to distribute them, and an apostle or angel of the congregation, called the *Scheliach tsibbur*, whose duty it was to conduct the synagogue worship, and to represent the congregation. So here the apostles desired the brethren to look out among them seven men of good report, full of the Holy Ghost and of wisdom, that is, of those who had received the gift of the Holy Ghost at Pentecost, whom they might appoint. And when the seven were selected they were set before the apostles: and when they had prayed, they laid their hands on them. This, then, was the first institution of a permanent ministry, consisting of seven Christian presbyters for the ministerial work of the Church; and as the seven Jewish presbyters were called the good men of the city, so, then, Christian presbyters were to be men of good report. And when Titus was organising the churches in Crete he was directed to ordain elders in every city.[6]

[6] English commentators, without an exception, regard this as the appointment of the order of deacons in the Church, in this following the view of the mediæval Church; but it was not till after the fourth century that this interpretation was put upon the incident by the Church, and adopted in appointing seven deacons in Rome. It seems strange, however, that St. Luke does not call them deacons, and throughout the whole narrative of the Acts of the Apostles nowhere mentions the separate order of deacons; while, on the other hand, he mentions the presbyters or elders of the Church at Jerusalem; and if these were not the elders, he nowhere mentions their institution.

Bishop Lightfoot, in his dissertation on the Christian ministry, treats this subject in a very perfunctory way. He admits that they are not called deacons, but that the words διακονειν and διακονία are repeated more than once; but these words were not used then in a restricted sense, but applied to the whole functions of the ministry, as is plain from the work reserved by the apostles being termed likewise διακονία.

The German commentators, as usual, take a more candid view of the passage, and are more free from ecclesiastical bias. Bishop Lightfoot says they do so from a strange perversity, and refers to Böhmer, Ritschl, and Lange as holding them to be presbyters; but he is obliged to admit that if St. Luke here records the first institution of the order of deacons, which does not again appear till later, and in connection with the Gentile-Christian Church, and are never mentioned again in the Acts, he is entirely silent as to the institution of the order of presbyters, who are frequently mentioned in the Acts of the Apostles.

Uhlhorn, in his treatise on Christian charity in the ancient Church, discusses this subject thoroughly, and shows that at this time the administration of alms, according to the express testimony of the Acts, was subsequently in the hands of the elders even in Jerusalem; and to this we may add the weighty authority of Dr. Döllinger, who in his *First Age of Christianity and the Church*, notwithstanding the view of his own Church, arrives at the same conclusion.

Soon after a third party was added to the Church, not of Hellenist Jews, but of Jews of Jerusalem, and consisting of those who had hitherto been its most strenuous opponents; for we are told that "*the word of God increased; and the number of the disciples multiplied in Jerusalem greatly: and a great company of the priests were obedient to the faith.*" These probably formed that Judaising party in the Church who maintained that it was necessary to keep the Law, and would impose it as a yoke upon all believers, against which St. Paul so strenuously protested.

The next great event in the history of the Jewish-Christian Church was the persecution which followed the martyrdom of St. Stephen, and their dispersion throughout the regions of Judea and Samaria, the apostles alone excepted. It is at this time that we must place the Epistle of St. James, which may be viewed as, with the exception of St. Matthew's Gospel, the document *par excellence* of the Jewish-Christian Church. The chief and most prominent man in the Church at Jerusalem was at this time, not St. James the Lord's brother, but the Apostle St. James, the son of Zebedee; for it was especially to please the Jews who opposed the Church that Herod stretched forth his hand to vex certain of the Church, and killed James the brother of John with the sword; and he would naturally select the head of the Church at Jerusalem for the purpose. If the Epistle was written at this time, it is to this James that, according to the early tradition of the Church, it must be ascribed; and the opening verses of the Epistle indicate this very clearly, when the Christian Jews of Jerusalem are said to be scattered abroad. The word used is διεσπόρησαν, and the Epistle is addressed to the twelve tribes, that is, the Jews generally, "*who are scattered abroad*" (ἐν τῇ διασπορᾷ); and the next verses refer manifestly to some great trial to which their faith had been exposed. Then the word used by St. James for a Christian assembly is synagogue, which is only appropriate to a Jewish-Christian Church still under the influence of Jewish customs; and St. James further refers to their ministers as the presbyters or elders of the Church,[7] and to their practice of the Jewish custom of anointing the sick with oil on the Sabbath day.

[7] When the Epistle of St. James was supposed to have been one of the later Epistles, it was naturally ascribed to the brother of our Lord at a time when he appears prominently in connection with the Church of Jerusalem; but it is now generally admitted that it is the earliest work of the New Testament, and must have been written before the Council of Jerusalem, and before the martyrdom of St. James the brother of St. John; and to him it was assigned by the early Church.

The oldest MSS. of the Peshito Syriac version state that it is an Epistle of "James the Apostle;" and the Carbey MS. of the New Testament has at the end of the Epistle, "Explicit Epistola Jacobi filii Zuebedei."

There is a Syriac note prefixed to the printed editions of the Syriac version of the Catholic Epistles, "We here print the three Epistles of James, Peter, and John, who were witnesses to the revelation of our Lord when He was transfigured;" and the title of "the Lord of glory," applied to Jesus in chap. ii. 1 is more appropriate in the mouth of the Apostle St. James, who witnessed His glory at the transfiguration, than in that of James the Lord's brother; while the numerous parallelisms between the Epistle and the Sermon on the Mount indicate one who was present and heard it.

As long as the Church existed in the main as a Jewish-Christian Church, we find this distinction between the missionary and ministerial functions of its clergy preserved. We see the apostles as missionaries or evangelists preaching the gospel, first to the Jews and after to the Gentiles; and when they founded Churches, of which the main constituents were Jews, we see them ordaining presbyters or elders in every Church for the work of the ministry; and at the Council of Jerusalem we see the two bodies distinguished from each other when the decree adopted at that assembly is issued by the apostles and elders. Now, as the Church begins to be more and more influenced by the infection of Gentile members, we see the term pastors ($\pi o \iota \mu \acute{\epsilon} \nu o \varsigma$) applied to those who were rulers, and afterwards that of bishops. Thus in the Epistle to St. Timothy, read in the purely Gentile Churches such as that of Philippi, the body of elders fall into two divisions—bishops, who represented the *Scheliach tsibbur*, who appears in the Book of Revelations as the Angel of the Church, and the three rulers of the synagogue; and deacons, who represented the three *Parnasim;* while in the end of the first century the term bishop is confined to the president or $\pi\rho\omega\eta\sigma\tau\omega\varsigma$ of the body, and that of presbyters applied to three rulers of the Church.

The word *diakonia*, too, underwent a similar change. It is first applied to the entire ministry of the Church before any distinction was made between its missionary and its ministerial functions. It is then restricted to the ministerial work of the Church, as in Rom. xvi. 3, where prophecy and teaching is distinguished from *diakonia* or ministering; and in Eph. iv. 12, where the perfecting of the saints and the edifying or building up of the body of Christ is distinguished from the work of the ministry (εἰς ἔργον διακονίας); and finally it was restricted to the function of the deacons.[8]

An important question still remains for our consideration, viz. how far the ritual of the early Christian Church was affected by that of the synagogue or of the temple, and to what extent it is represented by any of the early liturgical forms that have been preserved. It seems, however, obvious that after the effusion of the Holy Ghost at Pentecost, and while the disciples were still full of the Holy Spirit, there could have been no fixed form of prayer, but they must have prayed as the Spirit gave them utterance. Thus St. Peter refers to the words of Joel the prophet, "*I will pour out my Spirit in these days, and they shall pro-*

---

[8] These numbers appear in the Apostolical Constitutions of the Church of Alexandria.

ON THE ORDAINING OF ELDERS.

2. The bishop is to ordain two elderly men as elders, or rather three, both to support the bishop and to make the people love their shepherd. In particular, one is to have the care of the altar and of those who belong to it, the other of the wants of the people.—Can. 17-19.

ON THE APPOINTMENT OF DEACONS.

3. Three men at least are to certify to their godly life in having had one wife, and brought up their children well. They are to care for the poor by watching the rich contribute to their necessities.—Can. 20.

phesy," that is, praise God; and this seems to be implied by the expression that they prayed "with one accord." Though there could not have been a fixed form of words in prayer at this time, Probst makes the very just remark that a fixed form and settled order undoubtedly characterised the apostolic divine service. God is not a God of disorder, therefore everything must be done with propriety and order. We have seen that the disciples went to the temple at the hour of prayer according to the usual custom of the Jews, but this was private prayer uttered during the time of the sacrifice: and there, too, they preached the gospel; but this was missionary work. But when the Christians met for their own peculiar worship it was at home, that is, in their private places of meeting. Besides the temple worship, which could only be carried on by their living in Jerusalem, the regular worship of Jews over the whole country was that in the synagogue. It was a liturgical service, and commenced with the prayer called the *Kaddish*, the model in which the Lord's Prayer was evidently formed, adapting it to the use of the disciples. This was followed by the *Schemah* or Confession of Faith, and after that the *Schemen Esre* or nineteen prayers. Each prayer was repeated, first in silence by each member of the congregation, and then aloud by the *Scheliach tsibbur*, the people answering Amen after each. It was preceded by the versicles, "O Lord, open my lips: and my mouth shall show forth Thy praise." The *Kaddish* was again repeated, and then followed the reading of the Law. After this the 145th Psalm and the reading of a portion of the Prophets. Then the *Duraschoth* or discourse, and the service closed by the *Kaddish* being again repeated.

We do not find in the apostolic age any direct evidence in the New Testament that this precise order was followed. But there are indications that each part of it formed a portion of the Christian service; though while the disciples were still under the influence of the Pentecostal effusion, and full of the Holy Ghost, the words of the prayer must have been such as the Holy Spirit at the time gave them utterance. Then we find that when Peter and John were brought before the High Priests and elders for preaching in the temple, and dismissed, they went to their own company, that is, the disciples assembled at home, and "*they lifted up their voice to God with one accord;*" and "*when they had prayed, the place was shaken where they were assembled together; and they were all filled with the Holy Ghost*" (Acts iv. 31). Then we gather from the First Epistle to the Corinthians that there was at this time a formal creed, when St. Paul tells the Corinthians that he delivered unto them first of all that which he also received, how that "*Christ died for our sins according to the Scriptures; and that He was buried; and that He rose again the third day*" (xv. 3, 4); and the elements of their worship are implied in his direction to Timothy to "*give heed to reading, to exhortation, to teaching.*"

But there was one important addition to this service,

viz. the daily breaking of bread; and the Christian worship must therefore have centred around the celebration of the Eucharist. And here we have more direct indications that though the prayers were at this time extemporary, the form of the service was in every respect analogous to the ritual of the Passover supper when the Eucharist was instituted.

When the Passover was instituted this injunction was given to the Israelites, "*This day shall be unto you for a memorial; and ye shall keep it a feast to the Lord throughout your generations: ye shall keep it a feast by an ordinance for ever. Seven days shall ye eat unleavened bread; even the first day ye shall put away leaven out of your houses*" (Ex. xii. 14, 15). But St. Paul applies this description to the Christian celebration of the Eucharist, giving a spiritual meaning to the words when he says, "*Purge out therefore the old leaven, that ye may be a new lump, as ye are unleavened. For even Christ our Passover is sacrificed for us: therefore let us keep the feast, not with old leaven, neither with the leaven of malice and wickedness; but with the unleavened bread of sincerity and truth*" (1 Cor. v. 7, 8).

Then at the second part of the Passover supper, when the dishes which had been removed are brought back and placed on the table, the master of the household uttered the general thanksgiving, beginning, "Therefore are we bound to give thanks, to praise, to laud, to glorify, to extol, to honour, to magnify Him that hath done for our fathers and for us all these wonders;

who hath brought us from bondage to freedom, from sorrow to rejoicing, from mourning to a good day, from darkness to a great light, from affliction to redemption;" and the feast ended with a song of praise, in the end of which was the sentence, "Blessed be Thou, O Lord the King, who art to be lauded with praises;" to which those present responded with "Amen." St. Paul evidently refers to a similar thanksgiving uttered in the spirit when he says in the First Epistle to the Corinthians, after he had described to them the proper mode of celebrating the Lord's Supper, "*I will pray with the spirit, and I will pray with the understanding also; I will sing with the spirit, and I will sing with the understanding also. Else, when thou shalt bless with the spirit* (εὐλογῆς), *how shall he that occupieth the room of the unlearned say Amen at thy giving of thanks*" (εὐχαριστίᾳ.) Here the two Greek words εὐλογῆς and εὐχαριστίᾳ are used synonymously for the same prayer of thanksgiving.

Now, when at the Passover supper the master of the household breaks the cake of unleavened bread and distributes it, he gives thanks thus, "Blessed be Thou, O Lord our God, King everlasting, who hath sanctified us by Thy commandments, and commanded us concerning the eating of unleavened bread;" and when he gives the cup he likewise gives thanks over it, thus, "Blessed be Thou, O Lord, who hast created the fruit of the vine." So St. Paul tells us that our Saviour took bread, and when "*He had given thanks* (εὐχαριστήσας) *He brake it;*" and "*after the same manner also He took the cup.*" This is the oldest account we have of the institution of the Lord's Supper; but when given by the evangelists we find St. Matthew and St. Mark used the word εὐλογησας, but St. Luke has the word εὐχαρίστησας. The use of the former word shows that the form of the thanksgiving must have been the same, and must have commenced with the "Blessed be Thou, O God."

Then, when St. Paul says in chap. x., "*The cup of blessing which we bless, is it not the communion of the blood of Christ? The bread which we break, is it not the communion of the body of Christ?*" Taken in connection with the description in the following chapter, it is plain that the repetition by the officiating minister of the words of institution was the form of consecration of the elements.

The document termed the "Teaching of the Twelve Apostles," which undoubtedly belongs to the latter part of this century, shows us the transition from the prayers uttered in the spirit to a fixed form. A form of words for the blessing or thanksgiving for the cup and the bread are given, and the order is the same as in the tenth chapter of the First Epistle to the Corinthians. This form is based upon the words of the blessing or thanksgiving in the Passover ritual. In chap. ix. we read, "Now, as regards the Eucharist, give thanks (εὐχαριστησατε) after this manner. First for the cup: We give thanks to Thee, our Father, for the holy vine of David, Thy servant, which Thou hast made known to us through Jesus Thy servant: to Thee be the glory for ever. And for the broken bread: We give thanks to Thee, our Father, for the life and knowledge which Thou hast made known to us through Jesus Thy servant: to Thee be the glory for ever." And the celebration was followed by a general thanksgiving for all God's mercies, spiritual and temporal, with a prayer for the Church universal. The transition from a time when these thanksgivings were uttered in such words as the Spirit suggested is indicated by the concluding words of this chapter: " But permit the prophets to give thanks (εὐχαριστειν) as much or in what words they wish;" and in a following chapter a prophet is defined as one " who speaks in the Spirit."

The oldest detailed descriptions we have of the early Christian service is that given us by Justin Martyr, who wrote in the first half of the second century. He tells us that "on the day called Sunday all who live in cities or in the country gather together to one place (ἐπὶ τὸ αὐτό),[9] and the memoirs of the apostles (which in a preceding chapter Justin says are called Gospels), or the writings of the prophets, are read as long as time permits; then, when the reader has ceased, the president (προεστως) verbally instructs and exhorts to the imitation of these good things. Then we all rise together and pray." This, it will be seen, is exactly analogous to the service of the synagogue, and contains precisely the same elements. This is then followed by

[9] This is the same expression as is used for the place of assembly in the Acts of the Apostles.

the celebration of the Eucharist. "When our prayer is ended, bread and wine and water are brought, and the president, in like manner, offers prayers according to his ability, and the people assent, saying 'Amen.'" This is obviously the Eucharistic prayer referred to in the chapter of the First Epistle to the Corinthians; and the expression "according to his ability," or rather power (ὅση δύναμις αὐτῷ), again indicates the transition from prayer in the spirit to a fixed form. If his possession of the spirit gave him the power, he prayed in the spirit; if not, he used a fixed form; and then there is a distribution to each, and a participation of that over which thanks have been given. In the previous chapter he mentions that this food had been blessed, that is, consecrated, by the prayer of his word. And after that follows the distribution of alms, or the κοινωνία, showing the connection of the latter with the breaking of bread, as indicated in the second chapter of the Acts of the Apostles. This account is taken from his first *Apology*, chap. 67; but the celebration of the Eucharist is also referred to in his *Dialogue with Trypho*, chap. 117, where he explains in what sense it was a sacrifice. He says "that prayers and giving of thanks, when offered by worthy men, are the only perfect and well-pleasing sacrifices to God. For such alone Christians have undertaken to offer, and in the remembrance effected by their solid and liquid food, whereby the suffering of the Son of God which He endured is brought to mind." It is reasonable to suppose that the service he here describes was that of the city in which he generally dwelt, and in his *Dialogue with Trypho* he mentions the city he was there in as "our city." That city, however, was undoubtedly Ephesus.[10]

The oldest account we have of the earliest written Liturgies is in the tract entitled "Treatise regarding the Tradition of the Divine Liturgy, attributed to Poclus, Bishop of Constantinople in A.D. 437." It commences thus: "Many, indeed, and other pastors and doctors of the holy Church, who succeeded the holy apostles, have delivered in writing an edition of the very holy Liturgy, of whom the first and most distinguished were considered the blessed Clement, the disciple and successor of the chief prince of the apostles, who transcribed it as dictated to him by the holy apostles and the holy teachers; who was elected by lot, and appointed by the High Priest, Christ our God, the first Bishop of the Church of Jerusalem. Then Basil the Great, observing the indolence and laziness of men, and that they thought of nothing but what was earthly and base, curtailed the length of the Liturgy, not because he thought there was

---

[10] Eusebius, in the 18th chapter of his fourth book, distinctly says that he had his conference with Trypho in the city of Ephesus, and what he tells us of it in this dialogue confirms it. He says in chap. 1 that "he was going about one morning in the walks of Xystus," and this Xystus was at Ephesus. Then, that "he used to go into a certain field not far from the sea," which also indicates Ephesus. Eusebius tells us that he was martyred in Rome; and he probably alludes to his journey from Ephesus to Rome when Trypho closes the dialogue by saying, "You are on the eve of departure, and expect daily to set sail."

anything superfluous, or that it contained too much, but that he might put an end to the laziness and slovenliness both of those who prayed and who listened ; and, moreover, as much might be compressed into the same time, published a shorter form."

The oldest Liturgy is here said to be that attributed to St. Clement ; and it is undoubtedly the Liturgy in the eighth book of the *Apostolical Constitutions*, usually called the Clementine. Poclus adds, however, that in these Liturgies a new prayer had been inserted. He says, " By their prayers they besought the Holy Spirit to come, that His divine presence should reveal the bread offered in sacrifice and the wine mingled with water as the actual body and the actual blood of our Saviour Jesus Christ, and manifest the consecration, which holy rite is indeed observed to the present day, and will be observed to the end of time."

St. Basil fully admits that this was a new prayer inserted after the apostolic age, when he says, "The words of the Epiclesis or Invocation at the displaying or dedicating of the bread of thanksgiving and the cup of blessing—which of the saints left behind for us in writing ? For, you know, we are not content with the things which the apostle or the Gospel relates, but we prefix and suffix other expressions, which we regard as highly important for the mystery, having them handed down to us from unwritten tradition."

This prayer, termed the Epiclesis or Invocation, was, however, originally connected, not with the consecration of the elements, but with the communion, as is apparent from the language which appears, from the tract attributed to Proclus, to have been at first used. St. Paul, in the eleventh chapter of the First Epistle to the Corinthians, had warned communicants against "eating this bread and drinking this cup unworthily." "*For*," he says, "*he that eateth and drinketh unworthily, eateth and drinketh damnation, or rather judgment, unto himself, not discerning the Lord's body.*" And the teaching of the twelve apostles also gives this warning, "If any one is holy, let him come. If any one is not holy, let him repent. Maranatha (the Lord cometh). Amen."

These warnings led to a special prayer for the descent of the Holy Spirit "to reveal the elements as the actual body and the actual blood of our Saviour Jesus Christ, and manifest the consecration," that is, to enable the communicants to discern the Lord's body.

The same expressions are used in the Clementine Liturgy and that of St. Basil; and the natural inference from the words of Proclus is that they were originally in the Liturgy of St. James likewise.

The Clementine Liturgy, which, according to Proclus, was the oldest and first written Liturgy, shows that it still bore evidence of Jewish influence in the long detail given in the Eucharistic prayer of the events in the Old Testament in which the interposition of the Almighty was manifested.

Probst considers that the Clementine Liturgy was undoubtedly used in the Church of Antioch till it was superseded by the Liturgy of St. Basil, and was, in fact, the Liturgy of that Church; and he points out two remarkable features which characterise it. First, that much of the language used in the Eucharistic prayer corresponds in a remarkable degree with the language of Justin Martyr; and secondly, that the Liturgy as it appears in the eighth book of the *Apostolical Constitution* has been transcribed from two different editions of it. They appear to have corresponded in the Anaphora down to the end of the oblation, and it is then followed by two different forms of the Epiclesis or Invocation and the intercessory prayers. One of these forms, however, is undoubtedly connected with the Church of Antioch, for St. Chrysostom, in his Homily on Eustathius, Bishop of Antioch about 330, says that great and pious man thought the very Liturgy of his Church clearly taught him that it was his duty to include the whole Church in his solicitude. For he says thus, "If we must pray *for the universal Church which extends itself from one end of the inhabited globe to the other*, it is still more our duty to show that we care for the whole of it." And the expression underlined occurs only in one of the intercessory prayers of this Liturgy. The other form seems to have belonged to the form used in the Church of Ephesus, as Irenæus, whose notice of the Eucharistic service probably referred to that used at Ephesus, indicates that a similar form was used there when he says, referring to the oblation, "Thus it is therefore also His will that we too should offer a gift at the altar frequently and without intermission. The altar, then, is in heaven (for towards that place are our prayers and oblations directed);" the temple likewise (is there), as John says in the Apocalypse, "*And the temple of God was opened;*" the tabernacle also, "*For behold,*" he says, "*the tabernacle of God, in which He will dwell with men*" (xxi. 3); and this he calls the Ekklesis or Evocation of God.

The following is the Anaphora of the Clementine Liturgy, in which the expressions corresponding with those of Justin Martyr are indicated, and the two forms of Epiclesis and intercessory prayer placed in parallel columns:—

Anaphora of the Clementine Liturgy.[11]

The bishop—
Lift up your mind.
All the people—
We lift it up unto the Lord.
The bishop—
Let us give thanks to the Lord.
All the people—
It is meet and right so to do.
Then let the bishop say—
It is very meet and right before all things to sing an hymn to Thee, who art the true God, who art before all beings, from whom the whole family in heaven and earth is named, *who only art unbegotten and without*

[11] Preface and Thanksgiving Prayer.

beginning, and without a ruler and without a master; who standest in need of nothing; *who art the bestower of everything that is good; who art beyond all cause and generation; who art always and immutably the same; from whom all things came into being, as from their proper original.*[12] For Thou art eternal knowledge, everlasting sight, unbegotten hearing, untaught wisdom, the first by nature and the measure of being, and beyond all number; who didst bring all things out of nothing into being by Thy only-begotten Son, *but didst beget Him before all ages by Thy will, Thy power*, and Thy goodness, without any instrument. *The only-begotten Son, God the Word, the living Wisdom, the First-born of every creature, the Angel of Thy great counsel; and Thy High Priest, but the King and Lord*[13] of every intellectual and sensible nature, who was before all things, *by whom were all things. For Thou, O eternal God, didst make all things by Him,* and through Him it is that Thou vouchsafest Thy suitable providence over the whole world; for by the very same that Thou bestowedst being, didst Thou also bestow wellbeing; the God and Father of Thy only-begotten Son, *who by Him didst make before all things the cherubim and the seraphim, the æons and hosts, the powers and authorities, the principalities and thrones, the archangels and angels: and after all these didst by Him make this visible world, and all things that are therein.*[14] For Thou art He who didst frame the heaven as an arch, and stretch it out

[12] Justin, *Dialogue with Trypho.*   [13] *Ibid.*   [14] *Ibid.*

like the covering of a tent, and didst found the earth upon nothing by Thy mere will; who didst fix the firmament and prepare the night and the day; who didst bring the light out of Thy treasures, and on its departure didst bring on darkness, for the rest of the living creatures that move up and down in the world; who didst appoint the sun in heaven to rule over the day, and the moon to rule over the night, and didst inscribe in heaven the choir of stars to praise Thy glorious majesty; who didst make the water for drink and for cleansing; the air, in which we live, for respiration and the affording of sounds, by means of the tongue, which strikes the air, and the hearing, which co-operates therewith, so as to perceive speech when it is received by it, and falls upon it; who madest fire for our consolation in darkness, for the supply of our want, and that we might be warmed and enlightened by it; who didst separate the great sea from the land, and didst render the former navigable and the latter fit for walking, and didst replenish the former with small and great living creatures, and filledst the latter with the same, both tame and wild; didst furnish it with various plants and crown it with herbs, and beautify it with flowers and enrich it with seeds; who didst ordain the great deep, and on every side madest a mighty cavity for it, which contains seas of salt waters heaped together, yet didst Thou every way bound them with barriers of the smallest sand; who sometimes dost raise it to the height of mountains by the winds, and sometimes doth smooth it into a plain; sometimes dost enrage it with a tempest, and sometimes dost still it with a calm, that it may be easy to seafaring men in their voyages; who didst encompass this world, which was made by Thee through Christ, with rivers, and water it with currents, and moisten it with springs that never fail, and didst bind it round with mountains for the immovable, and secure consistence of the earth; for Thou hast replenished Thy world, and adorned it with sweet-smelling and with healing herbs, with many and various living creatures, strong and weak, for food and for labour, tame and wild; with the noises of creeping things, the sounds of various sorts of flying creatures; with the circuits of the years, the number of months and days, the order of the seasons, the courses of the rainy clouds, for the production of the fruits and the support of living creatures. Thou hast also appointed the station of the winds, which blow when commanded by Thee, and the multitude of the plants and herbs. And Thou hast not only created the world itself, but hast also made man for a citizen of the world, exhibiting him as the ornament of the world; *for Thou didst say to Thy Wisdom, " Let us make man according to our image and according to our likeness;"* [15] and let them have dominion over the fish of the sea and over the fowls of the heaven. Wherefore also Thou hast made him of an immortal soul, and of a body liable to dissolution,—the former out of nothing, the latter out of the

[15] Justin, *Dial.* c. 61.

four elements,—*and hast given him as to his soul rational knowledge, the discerning of piety and impiety, and the observation of right and wrong; and as to his body Thou hast granted him five senses and progressive motion;* [16] for Thou, O God Almighty, didst by Thy Christ plant a paradise in Eden, in the east adorned with all plants fit for food, and didst introduce him into it as into a rich banquet. And when Thou madest him *Thou gavest him a law implanted within him, that so he might have at home and within himself the seed of divine knowledge;* [17] and when Thou hadst brought him into the paradise of pleasure, Thou allowed him the privilege of enjoying all things, only forbidding the tasting of one tree, in hopes of greater blessings; that in case he would keep that command, he might receive the reward of it, which was immortality. But when he neglected that command, and tasted of the forbidden fruit by the seduction of the serpent and the counsel of his wife, Thou didst justly cast him out of paradise. Yet of Thy goodness Thou didst not overlook him, nor suffer him to perish utterly, for he was Thy creature; but Thou didst subject the whole creation to him, and didst grant him liberty to procure himself food by his own sweat and labours, whilst Thou didst cause all the fruits of the earth to spring up, to grow, and to ripen. But when Thou hadst laid him asleep for a while, Thou didst with an oath call him to a restoration again, didst loose the bond of death, and promise him life after

[16] Justin, *Apol.* ii. c. 7. *Ib. Dial.* c. 62.   [17] *Ib. Apol.* ii. c. 8.

the resurrection. And not this only, but when Thou hadst increased his prosperity to an innumerable multitude, those that continued with Thee Thou didst glorify, and those who did apostatise from Thee Thou didst punish. And while Thou didst accept of the sacrifice of Abel as of an holy person, Thou didst reject the gift of Cain, the murderer of his brother, as of an abhorred wretch, and besides these, Thou didst accept of Seth and Enos, and didst translate Enoch; for Thou art the Creator of men, and the giver of life, and the supplier of wants, and the giver of laws, and the rewarder of those that observe them, and the avenger of those that transgress them; who didst bring the great flood upon the world by reason of the multitude of the ungodly, and didst deliver righteous Noah from that flood by an ark, with eight souls, the end of the foregoing generations and the beginning of those that were to come; who didst kindle a fearful fire against the five cities of Sodom, and didst turn a fruitful land into a salt lake for the wickedness of them that dwelt therein, but didst snatch holy Lot out of the conflagration. Thou art He who did deliver Abraham from the impiety of his forefathers, and didst appoint him to be the heir of the world, and didst discover to him Thy Christ; who didst aforehand ordain Melchisedek an high priest for Thy worship; who didst render Thy patient servant Job the conqueror of that serpent who is the patron of wickedness; who madest Isaac the son of the promise, and Jacob the father of twelve sons, and didst increase his posterity to a multitude, and bring him into Egypt with seventy-five souls. Thou, O Lord, didst not overlook Joseph, but grantedst him, as a reward of his chastity for Thy sake, the government over the Egyptians. Thou, O Lord, didst not overlook the Hebrews when they were afflicted by the Egyptians on account of the promises made to their fathers; but Thou didst deliver them, and punish the Egyptians. And when men had corrupted the law of nature, and had sometimes esteemed the creation the effect of chance, and sometimes honoured it more than they ought and equalled it to the God of the universe, Thou didst not, however, suffer them to go astray, but didst raise up Thy holy servant Moses, and by him didst give the written law for the assistance of the law of nature, and didst show that the creation was Thy work, and didst banish away the error of polytheism. Thou didst adorn Aaron and his posterity with the priesthood, and didst punish the Hebrews when they sinned and received them again when they returned to Thee. Thou didst punish the Egyptians with a judgment of ten plagues, and didst divide the sea, and bring the Israelites through it, and drown and destroy the Egyptians who pursued after them. Thou didst sweeten the bitter water with wood; Thou didst bring water out of the rock of stone; Thou didst rain manna from heaven and quails, as meat out of the air; Thou didst afford them a pillar of fire by night to give them light, and a pillar of a cloud by day to overshadow them from the heat; Thou didst declare Joshua to be the general of the army, and didst overthrow the seven nations of Canaan by him; Thou didst divide Jordan and dry up the rivers of Etham; Thou didst overthrow walls without instruments or the hand of man. For all these things, glory be to Thee, O Lord Almighty.

(*Trisagion.*) Thee do innumerable hosts of angels, archangels, thrones, dominions, principalities, authorities, and powers Thine everlasting armies adore. The cherubim and the six-winged seraphim with twain covering their feet, with twain their heads, and with twain flying say, together with thousand thousands of archangels, and ten thousand times ten thousand of angels, incessantly and with constant and loud voices, and let all the people say with them, "Holy, holy, holy, Lord of hosts, heaven and earth are full of His glory: be Thou blessed for ever, Amen."

And afterward let the bishop say, For Thou art truly holy and most holy, the highest and most highly exalted for ever. Holy also is *Thy only-begotten Son, our Lord and God, Jesus Christ,*[18] *who in all things ministered to His God and Father, both in Thy various creation and Thy suitable providence, and has not overlooked lost mankind. But after the law of nature, after the exhortations in the positive law, after the prophetical reproofs and the government of the angels, when men had perverted both the positive law and that of nature, and had cast out of their mind the memory of the flood, the*

---

[18] Justin, *Apol.* i. c. 13.

burning of Sodom, the plagues of the Egyptians, and the slaughter of the inhabitants of Palestine, and being just ready to perish universally after an unparalleled manner, He was pleased by Thy goodwill to become man, who was man's Creator; to be under the laws, who was the Legislator; to be a sacrifice, who was an High Priest; to be a sheep, who was the Shepherd. And He appeased Thee, His God and Father, and reconciled Thee to the world, and freed all men from the wrath to come, and was made of a virgin, and was in flesh, being God the Word, the beloved Son, the first-born of the whole creation, and was, according to the prophecies which were foretold concerning Him by Himself, of the seed of David and Abraham, of the tribe of Judah. And He was made in the womb of a virgin, who formed all mankind that are born into the world; He took flesh, who was without flesh; He who was begotten before time, was born in time; He lived holily and taught according to the law; *He drove away every sickness and every disease from men;* and wrought signs and wonders among the people; and He was partaker of meat, and drink, and sleep, who nourishes all that stand in need of food, and fills every living creature with His goodness; He manifested His name to those who knew it not; He drove away ignorance; He revived piety, and fulfilled Thy will; He finished the work which Thou gavest Him to do; and when He had set all these things right, He was seized by the hands of the ungodly, of the High Priests and priests, falsely so called, and of the disobedient people, by the betraying of him, who was possessed of wickedness as with a confirmed disease; He suffered many things from thence, and endured all sorts of ignominy by Thy permission; He was delivered to Pilate the governor, and He that was the Judge was judged, and He that was the Saviour was condemned; He that was impassible was nailed to the cross, and He who was by nature immortal died, and *He that is the giver of life was buried, that He might loose those for whose sake He came from suffering and death, and might break the bonds of the devil and deliver mankind from his deceit.* He arose from the dead the third day; and when He had continued with His disciples forty days, He was taken up into the heavens, and is set down on the right hand of Thee, who art His God and Father.

(*Consecration.*) *Being mindful, therefore, of those things that He endured for our sakes, we give Thee thanks, O God Almighty, not in such manner as we ought, but as we are able, and fulfil His constitution.*[19] For in the same night that He was betrayed He took bread in His holy and undefiled hands, and, looking up to Thee, His God and Father, He brake it and gave it to His disciples, saying, This is the mystery of the new Covenant; take of it and eat. This is my body, which is broken for many for the remission of sins. In like manner also He took the cup and mixed it of wine and water, and sanctified it, and delivered it to them, saying, Drink ye all of this; for this is my blood which is shed

[19] Justin, *Apol.* i. c. 18.

for many for the remission of sins; do this in remembrance of me. For as often as ye eat this bread, and drink this cup, ye do show forth my death until I come.

(*Anemnesis and Oblation.*) Being mindful, therefore, of His passion and death, and resurrection from the dead, and return into the heavens, and His future second appearing wherein He is to come with glory and power to judge the quick and the dead, and to recompense to every one according to his works, we offer to Thee, our King and our God, according to His constitution, this bread and this cup, giving Thee thanks, through Him, that Thou hast thought us worthy to stand before Thee and to sacrifice to Thee; and we beseech Thee that Thou wilt mercifully look down upon these gifts, which we here set before Thee, O Thou God, who standest in need of none of our offerings.

(*Epiclesis.*) And do Thou accept them, to the honour of Thy Christ, and send down upon this sacrifice Thine Holy Spirit, the witness of the Lord Jesus' sufferings, that He may show this bread to be the body of Thy Christ, and the cup to be the blood of Thy Christ, that those who are partakers thereof may be strengthened for piety,

(*Ekklesis.*) Let us still further beseech God through His Christ, and let us beseech Him on account of the gift which is offered to the Lord God, that the good God will accept it, through the mediation of His Christ, upon His heavenly altar for a sweet-smelling savour.

may obtain the remission of their sins, may be delivered from the devil and his deceit, may be filled with the Holy Ghost, may be made worthy of Thy Christ, and may obtain eternal life upon Thy reconciliation to them, O Lord Almighty.

(*Intercession.*) *We further pray unto Thee, O Lord, for Thy holy Church, spread from one end of the world to another,*[20] which Thou hast purchased with the precious blood of Thy Christ, that Thou wilt preserve it unshaken and free from disturbance until the end of the world; for every episcopate which rightly divides the word of truth. We further pray to Thee, for me, who am nothing, who offer to Thee, for the whole presbytery, for the deacons and all

(omitted.)

(*Intercession.*) Let us pray for this Church and people. Let us pray for every episcopate, every presbytery, all the deacons and ministers in Christ, for the whole congregation, that the Lord will keep and preserve them all.

---

[20] Eustathius, Bishop of Antioch, A.D. 330.

the clergy, that Thou wilt make them wise and replenish them with the Holy Spirit. We further pray to Thee, O Lord, for the king and all in authority, for the whole army, that they may be peaceable towards us, that so, leading the whole time of our life in quietness and unanimity, we may glorify Thee through Jesus Christ, who is our hope. We further offer to Thee also for all those holy persons who have pleased Thee from the beginning of the world, patriarchs, prophets, righteous men, apostles, mentors, confessors, bishops, presbyters, deacons, subdeacons, readers, singers, virgins, widows, and lay persons, with all whose names Thou knowest. We further offer to Thee for this people, that Thou wilt render to them, to the

Let us pray for kings and those in authority, that they may be peaceable towards us, that so we may have and lead a quiet and peaceable life in all godliness and honesty.

Let us be mindful of the holy martyrs, that we may be thought worthy to be partakers of their trial. Let us pray for those that are departed in the faith.

praise of Thy Christ, a royal priesthood and an holy nation; for those that are in virginity and purity; for the widows of the Church; for those in honourable marriage and childbearing; for the infants of Thy people— that Thou wilt not permit any of us to become castaways. We further beseech Thee also for this city and its inhabitants; for those that are sick; for those in bitter servitude; for those in banishments; for those in prison; for those that travel by water or by land; that Thou, the helper and assister of all men, wilt be their supporter. We further also beseech Thee for those that hate us and persecute us for Thy name's sake; for those that are without, and wander out of the way; that Thou wilt convert them to goodness and pacify their anger.

We further also beseech Thee for the catechumens of the Church, and for those that are vexed by the adversary, and for our brethren the penitents, that Thou wilt perfect the first in the faith, that Thou wilt deliver the second from the energy of the evil one, and that Thou wilt accept the repentance of the last, and forgive both them and us our offences. We further offer to Thee also for the good temperature of the air and the fertility of the fruits, that so partaking perpetually of the good things derived from Thee we may praise Thee without ceasing, who givest food to all flesh. We further beseech Thee also for those who are absent on a good cause, that Thou wilt keep us in

Let us pray for the good temperature of the air and the perfect maturity of the fruits. Let us pray for those that are wisely enlightened, that they may be strengthened in the faith, and all may be mutually comforted by one another. Raise us up, O God, by Thy grace. Let us stand up and dedicate ourselves to God through His Christ.

And let the bishop say, O God, who art great and whose name is great, who art great in counsel and mighty in works, the God and Father of Thy holy child Jesus, our Saviour, look down upon us and all piety, and gather us together in the kingdom of Thy Christ, the God of all sensible and intelligent nature, our King, that Thou wouldst keep us immovable, unblamable, and unreprovable; for to Thee belongs all glory and worship, and thanksgiving, honour, and adoration, the Father, with the Son, and to the Holy Ghost, both now, and always, and for everlasting, and endless ages for ever.

And let all the people say, Amen.[21]

And let the bishop say, The peace of God be with you all.

And let all the people say, And with thy spirit.

upon this Thy flock, which Thou hast chosen by Him to the glory of Thy name; and sanctify our body and soul, and grant us the favour to be made pure from all filthiness of the flesh and spirit, and may obtain the good things laid up for us; and do not account any of us unworthy; but be Thou our comforter, helper, and protector through Thy Christ, with whom glory, honour, praise, doxology, and thanksgiving be to Thee and to the Holy Ghost for ever. Amen.

[21] Austin.

AUTHOR'S PREFACE.

IN order that the reader may not find himself alarmed, or perplexed by the multitude of details which we are compelled by the nature of the subject to bring before him, it may be as well to state shortly the most important and decisive results of them.

It is, of course, known that our Saviour instituted the Eucharist during the celebration of the Passover. The Passover, however, had already a fixed and very complicated ritual, to which the drinking of four cups of wine especially belonged. Now it can be shown that Christ consecrated the fourth cup. Between the filling and mixing the fourth cup, which betokens the offertory, and the drinking of it, which was the celebration of the communion, the ritual of the Passover prescribed the recitation of several psalms and prayers. But as our Lord certainly followed the prescribed form in celebrating His last Passover, the preface and canon must, with the exception of the new words of consecration introduced by Him, have been upon the model of this part of the ceremonial, a proposition which is fully confirmed by a comparison of the oldest Liturgy with the Hallel. From this it follows that the formation of the Liturgy must have been made by such persons as were present at the institution of the Holy Eucharist, and therefore could strictly adhere to it.

This conclusion is evident enough, and will at length, in spite of many and strong adverse interests, receive recognition, and the more secondary point will be sooner disputed. We have attempted also to show that the pre-communion which precedes the offertorium is constructed on the model of the Sabbath-morning prayers already brought by the apostles in external and internal connection with the Liturgy properly so called. If the assent of the reader to this is rendered more difficult by the fact that we no longer possess the accordant Jewish Formulary in the precise form which it had in the apostolic age, still its agreement with the Christian form is too remarkable, and with that proved by such outward witnesses, that mere accidental coincidence cannot be assumed.

On account of the great practical importance of the subject, which we earnestly commend to the consideration of all who stand apart from the Church, it appeared to demand an exposition as generally understood as possible, which can easily be united with a careful use and actual production of the primitive sources.

AUTHOR'S INTRODUCTION.

THERE is hardly a branch of theological science which has till quite recently been brought to so little certain and recognised results as the history of the Christian Liturgy. This arose in the main from the practical necessity that the Catholic doctrine of the Holy Eucharist in the representative continuance and application of the sacrifice of Christ, in opposition to the Protestant polemic, should be shown to be the primitive Christian form. But in a period of more than three centuries little more was done than to collect the material, which recently from their great numbers, critical inquiry rather tended to confuse than to enlighten. For this whole period produced no other certain conclusion of chief importance except the propositions so clearly formalised by Renandot, that the use of the same Liturgy by the orthodox as well as by Monophysites of Syria and Egypt proved their existence at latest since the fifth century, and that the agreement of all these Liturgies in their order, and frequently even in their expression, implied their being founded upon one common apostolic basis.

If, in spite of the assertions of so many learned and acute inquirers, that the darkness which rests upon the origin and earliest development of the Christian Liturgy could not be further cleared away, the cause of this is to be found in a prejudice by which they deprived themselves of the only then existing primitive means to the restoration of the apostolic Eucharistic ritual. For they held that the Liturgy contained in the *Apostolical Constitutions* was not only, not an example of the fourth or possibly of the third century, but declared it most extraordinarily to be the composition of a private person, which nowhere and on no occasion came into use in the Church. Probst first, in his admirable work on the Liturgies of the first three Christian centuries, which appeared in 1870, thoroughly disproved that prejudiced opinion, and raised the history of the Liturgy from being a series of unsupported conjectures to an exact historic knowledge. He regarded the Liturgy of the *Apostolical Constitutions* as being in substance that which the apostles had formed, and during the first three centuries used in the whole Church with some small local peculiarities, and from which, in consequence of the liturgical revision of the fourth century, those rituals of the several ecclesiastical provinces which deviated from each other were developed.

Probst thoroughly succeeded in establishing that

the Fathers of the first three centuries in their Liturgic quotations and allusions throughout adhered closely to the Liturgy of the *Apostolical Constitutions;* on the other hand, the passages in the New Testament on which he founded were so uncertain and susceptible of so many meanings, that they could hardly convince an unwilling critic of the apostolic origin of this Liturgy. The object of the following treatise is to supply this defect, and to prevent the undoubted Apostolic origin of the Liturgy of the primitive Church remaining for the future, at least to candid inquirers, any longer an open question. We shall show that the primitive Christian Liturgy, which the *Apostolical Constitutions* have preserved to us in an almost entirely authentic form, is closely connected both in the order of its parts and even in its expressions with the ritual of the Jewish Passover supper, and that though the precommunion which is directly formed from the conclusion of the Sabbath-morning prayer approaches it only distantly, the Canon adheres in the smallest point to the Hallel recited over the fourth and last Passover cup. Further, it will be shown as the ground of this agreement that our Saviour actually completed the consecration at this part of the Passover ritual, and actually made the fourth cup the Eucharistic one, from which it follows incontestably that the primitive Christian Liturgy is closely conformed to the first Eucharist celebrated by Christ Himself after the Passover supper, and very soon after this first celebration must have been recorded by the Apostles.

Our inquiry will thus fall into three parts, of which the first will be the oldest undoubted form of the Christian celebration of the Lord's Supper, the second the Jewish Passover ritual as used in our Saviour's time, as also the Sabbath-morning prayer, while the third will show the agreement of that Christian Formulary with the Jewish, and the conclusions to be derived from it. By avoiding strange letters and irrelevant citations we hope to treat this subject in the interest of many readers, still we shall not omit to give those acquainted with the Jewish literature the means of testing our conclusions by references to its primary sources.

I.

THE PRIMITIVE CHRISTIAN LITURGY.

§ 1. The Liturgy of the Apostolical Constitutions.

It is no part of our purpose to enter at present into the controversy regarding the period when the *Apostolical Constitutions* were compiled, or the connection of its various component parts; and this is the less necessary as the Liturgy contained in this apocryphal work, which we, for shortness, in following the example of St. Proclus usually termed the Clementine, can be shown by the strongest external, as well as internal, evidences to be substantially Apostolic; and this witness from the answer to that critical question neither requires confirmation nor has to dread contradiction. It is sufficient here to remark that the *Apostolical Constitutions* contain a double description of the Eucharistic celebration, which constitutes the entire description— in this wise, that the one treats mainly of the lectionary, shortly notices the pre-communion, the Canon and communion being simply referred to; while the other, on the contrary, presents to us completely the entire ritual, with the exception of the introductory lessons. Out of both descriptions we shall here give a condensed glance over the entire Clementine Liturgy, in order to make what follows more clear.

The Liturgy begins at once with lessons from Holy Scripture, two from the Old Testament, one out of the Epistles in the New Testament, and one from the Gospels. The former were read by the Lector, but the Gospel, while all stood, by a Deacon. Between the Old and New Testament lessons the Cantor sings the psalms, at the conclusion of which the people respond with the antiphon. The sermon follows the Gospel, and then the faithful rise up and answer by a Kyrie Eleison to the call of the Deacon to pray for the kneeling Catechumens. Then the Deacon calls upon the Catechumens to pray for themselves, to rise up and with bowed heads to receive the blessing of the Bishop, which is given to them in the form of an intercession, and then the Catechumens depart out of the church. The same proceedings are then repeated for the Energumens, Competents, and Penitents. After all have departed except those faithful who are entitled to communicate, these kneel down, and respond with Kyrie Eleison to the calls by the deacon to pray for the whole Church, for the Episcopate, for Priests, Deacons, Lectors, Singers, Virgins, Widows, Orphans, Married persons, Ascetes, Almsgivers, and Offering-bringers, for Neophytes, Sick persons, and Travellers, for those condemned on account of their faith to imprisonment or labour in mines, for Enemies and persecutors, for Christian children, for Each other, and for each Christian soul. Then, at the call of the Deacon, they rise up and bow the head while the Bishop pronounces a benediction over them. After the Deacon has called upon them to pay attention, the Bishop says, "The peace of God be with you all;" to which the people answer, "And with thy spirit." The faithful, at the call of the Deacon, then give each other the kiss of peace. The Priests wash their hands, the Deacons bring bread, wine, and water to the altar, where, surrounded by his clergy, the Bishop stands in a gorgeous vestment and prays silently. Two Deacons, with peacock's feathers or other fans, drive the insects from the oblations. Then begins the Canon of the Eucharist. The Bishop signs himself with the sign of the cross, and blesses the people with Pauline salutation, "The grace of the Almighty God, and the love of our Lord Jesus Christ, and the communion of the Holy Ghost be with you all." The people respond, "And with thy spirit." Then the Bishop says, "Lift up your minds;" and the people, "We lift them up unto the Lord." The Bishop, "Let us give thanks unto the Lord;" the people, "It is meet and right so to do." Then there follows the long consecration prayer, beginning, "It is truly meet and right to thank and praise God for all His goodness, and in especial for the institution of the Holy Eucharist." Then God is praised for what He is, and for Himself as the absolute, the highest, the most perfect, and of necessity self-existent Being. Then praise and thanks is offered to

Him, in that, although in Himself perfectly blessed, and in want of nothing, He has, through His only-begotten Son, created the universe, the Holy Spirit, Heaven, Earth, Sun, Moon, Stars, the Elements, the Seas, Streams, Mountains, Plants, and all this for man created after His own image. But as man lost Paradise through his disobedience, God forsook him not entirely, but after He had allowed him for a time to rest in sleep, has called him by an oath to newness of life. And also among Adam's descendants has glorified the obedient, punished the disobedient, as may be seen in individuals from His dealings with Abel, Cain, Seth, Enoch, Noah, Lot, Abraham, Melchisedek, Job, Isaac, Jacob, Joseph, Moses, Aaron, and Joshua. Here is especially considered God's leadings of mankind through the Law and the Messianic promises, and in especial the plagues of Egypt, the Exodus of Israel from Egypt, the march through the Red Sea, the miracles in the wilderness, the siege of the Canaanites, and the entrance to the Promised Land. For all this, in union with Cherubim and Seraphim and all the Angelic host, is praise and thanks offered to God, in which the whole people unite, saying, "Holy, holy, holy is the Lord of hosts; heaven and earth are full of His glory. Glory be to God on high for ever and ever. Amen."

After this interlude, the Bishop begins, connecting it with the Trisagion, again with the praise of the Holiness of God and His Son Jesus Christ, who, in order to save the human race from eternal destruction, had compassion on them, and by His Incarnation, His life on earth, His suffering, His death, His Resurrection and Ascension, redeemed us. After the words, "Reflecting then on that which He has suffered for us, we thank Thee, Almighty God, not as we ought, but as we can, and fulfil His commands," follows the account of the Institution of the Holy Eucharist, with the Consecrating words, to which is added the reminder of St. Paul (1 Cor. ii. 26), as if spoken by Christ Himself. Then the Bishop thus proceeds, "Being mindful, therefore, of His passion and death, and resurrection from the dead and ascension to heaven, and the future second appearing, wherein He is to come with glory and power to judge the quick and the dead, and to recompense to every one according to his works, we offer to Thee, our King and God, according to His ordinance, this Bread and this Cup, giving Thee thanks through Him that Thou hast thought us worthy to stand before Thee and to serve Thee as Priests; and we beseech Thee that Thou, O God, who standest in no need of them, will mercifully look down upon these gifts which we set before Thee, and do Thou accept them to the honour of Thy Christ, and send down upon this offering Thy Holy Spirit, the witness of the sufferings of the Lord Jesus, that He may show this Bread to be the Body of Thy Christ, and this Cup to be the Blood of Thy Christ, that these who are partakers may be strengthened for piety, may obtain the remission of their sins, may be delivered from the Devil and his deceit, may be filled with the Holy Spirit, may be made worthy of Thy Christ, and may obtain eternal life, in that Thou hast reconciled them, O Lord Almighty."

The Bishop brings in the offerings for all the petitions recited by the Deacon in the ante-communion, to which there are added Intercessions for the emperor and all in authority, and for the army, the commemoration of the saints, and all departed faithful, the prayer for the Catechumens, Energumens, and Penitents, as well as the prayer for good weather and a rich harvest. He then closes the long eucharistic prayer with these words, "For to Thee belongs all glory, worship, and thanksgiving, honour, and adoration, the Father with the Son and the Holy Spirit, both now and always and for everlasting and endless ages for ever," to which the people respond with "Amen." After the conclusion of the Canon, the Bishop says, "The peace of God be with you all;" and the people answer, "And with thy spirit."

The Deacon now calls upon the people to pray for the Church, Clergy, and Laity, those in authority, Martyrs, and those deceased, and for a blessing on the harvest. Several recent liturgists are of opinion that this call of the Deacon, beginning with, "Let us once more and again," to which the people respond with Kyrie Eleison, is either a later interpolation, or a variation of the Intercession prayer by the Priest in the Canon taken from another manuscript. But this is impossible, as the "once more and again" of the Deacon is to be found at least in the Liturgy of St. James, and other Formularies related to it, in the same place; and, moreover, with the object of ensuring the attention of the people during the silent prayer of the Priest which accompanies the breaking of the Bread and mixing of the Cup.[22] It would be necessary also to assume that an ecclesiastical usage, common almost to the whole Eastern Church, had arisen from an accidental mistake of a single manuscript, which is not to be thought of.

After an Intercessory prayer, preparatory to the Communion, after the Deacon has summoned to attention, the Bishop cries, "Holy things for Holy persons;" to which the people answer, "There is one that is Holy, there is one Lord, one Jesus Christ, to the Glory of God the Father, blessed for ever. Amen. Glory to God in the highest; on earth peace, goodwill towards men. Hosanna to the Son of David. Blessed is He that cometh in the name of the Lord, God the Lord, and He has appeared to us. Hosanna in the highest."

The Bishop then gives the Communion to himself first, then the Clergy and people, with the words, "The Body of Christ;" which the recipients acknowledge with "Amen." The Deacon then gives the Cup, saying, "The Blood of Christ the Cup of life," responded to with "Amen." During the Communion, Ps. xxxiii. is sung.

---

[22] Towards the end of the eighth century a schism took place among the Jacobites, in which one party wished to set aside the silent prayer of the priest during the breaking as unquestionably Nestorian; but the other, on that very ground, caused it to be recited aloud, and placed it before the "once more and again," during which it was formerly said (Asseman., *Bibl. Orient.* ii. pp. 208, 341, 348).

After the conclusion of the psalm, the Deacon says, "Now that we have received the precious Body and the precious Blood of Christ, let us give thanks to Him who has thought us worthy to partake of these holy mysteries, and also beseech Him that it be not to us for condemnation, but to salvation, to the advantage of soul and body, to the preservation of piety, to the remission of sins, and to the life of the world to come. Let us stand up in the Grace of Christ; we will dedicate ourselves to the only-unbegotten God and His Christ." The Bishop then says a thanksgiving and intercessory prayer. After the Deacon has said, "Bow down to God and receive His blessing," the Bishop gives the benediction, and then the Deacon dismisses the assembly with the words, "Depart in peace."

It appears that in the earliest period of the Christian Church the Liturgy used at each celebration was almost entirely the same; and, with the exception of the Scripture lessons and psalm in the beginning, there was little alteration. But certainly on the anniversaries of the Martyrs, and those for the souls of deceased faithful, there would be a special reference to those for whom it was held. On Good Friday the kiss of peace was omitted, and probably the Alleluia was added to the psalms; according to Tertullian, confined in the Western Church to certain periods of the Church's year.

§ 2. THE OTHER LITURGIES.

All other Liturgies which are to be found in the Catholic Church or in these sects which preserved the liturgic unbroken succession, fall naturally into the following five typical groups:—

1. The Petrine or Roman Liturgy, which is most remote in form from the Clementine, and is characterised by regularly changing Prayers and Prefaces, by the giving of the kiss of peace first before the Communion, and by the position of a part of the Intercessory prayer before the Consecration.

2. The Gallican Liturgy, which apparently originating from Asia Minor, may be traced back to St. John,[23] stands nearer to the Oriental than to the Roman form. In this there is not only a change of Prayers and Prefaces, but also of the great part of the Canon. Instead of the Intercessory prayer after the Consecration, the Diptychs of the living and of the dead were read between the Offertorium and the kiss of peace, but the Mozarabic rite prescribes to the priest to introduce a silent *memento pro vivis* before the Lord's Prayer. In France this rite was set aside by Charlemagne.[24] It held its position longer in Spain, under the name of the Mozarabic, till Pope Gregory VII. prohibited it, though

---

[23] The Editor thinks it necessary to state here that he entirely differs from Professor Bickell in this opinion, which he has adopted from a conjecture of Palmer.

[24] What is now called the Gallican rite has nothing to do with this old Gallican Liturgy, but is based partly on a peculiar development

still preserved in a papal foundation of Cardinal Ximenes in a chapel of the Cathedral of Toledo.

3. The Liturgy of St. Mark, which until superseded by the Constantinopolitan Liturgy, was used by the orthodox in Egypt, and now under the name of the Liturgy of St. Cyril by the Monophysite Copts. It has the peculiarity that the Intercessory prayer is thrust into the Preface. This unusual arrangement is not to be found in the other two Coptic Liturgies, named of Gregorius and Basilius. The latter is the Norm of the three Coptic Liturgies, inasmuch as that all before and after the Anaphora (Canon) is only indicated. On the other hand, the Ethiopic Liturgy of all the Apostles, which is the Norm of the other sixteen Ethiopic Anaphoras, has likewise the Intercessory prayer before the Sanctus.

4. The East Syrian Liturgy, while originally at all events used by the Christians in Persia, perhaps also in Mesopotamia, remained later in use by the Nestorians only. Its Norm is the Liturgy of the holy apostles Adeus and Maris, the first bishops of Edessa and Seleucia, on the model which the Anaphora of Theodorus and of Nestorius were formed. The position of the Intercessory prayer invariably before the Invocation of the Holy Spirit is characteristic of this rite.

5. The Liturgy of St. James has at length spread of the Roman rite, partly on the arbitrary directions of more recent bishops. A few isolated parts, as, for instance, the episcopal consecration before the communion, have here and there been retained from the old Gallican rite.

from Jerusalem over nearly the whole of the East. For if the Greek form of the Liturgy of St. James has been for long almost entirely superseded by the Constantinopolitan rite, it still in its Syrian rendering serves the Jacobites and Maronites as a Norm from which not less than sixty-four other Anaphoras have been compiled. Still, however, the Liturgy of St. Basil, as well as its Elaboration and Norm, that of St. Chrysostom, which two are alone used in the Greek Church, as well as the ceremonies based upon the Liturgy of St Basil, are to be viewed as revisions of the Liturgy of St. James. It, however, has itself among them all the greatest resemblance with the Clementine, as it and all derived from it places the Intercessory prayer after the Invocation of the Holy Spirit.

That the Liturgies of the Churches of Rome, France, Alexandria, Seleucia, Jerusalem, and Constantinople had their present form in the main as far back as the fifth century, can be distinctly proved. In the West, liturgic manuscripts are not awanting which reach back to that age and afford a documentary proof of the above assertion.

The oldest document containing the Roman rite is a Sacramentarium discovered by Branchini in a Veronese manuscript of the end of the fifth or beginning of the sixth century, from which we can very clearly ascertain the position of the Roman Liturgy in the fifth century before the Gelasian reform. It contains merely those portions which varied with each festival, and consists of a number of Collects, Secreta, Prefaces, Postcommunions, and Benedictions; for at an early period both Prefaces and Benedictions were different in each service, while at present the former varies only eleven times, and the latter never changes. That the Canon of the then Roman Mass was the same as the present, is evident from the additions to the Canon on certain festivals which are in part *verbatim* the same as we find in the present Roman Missal. In this way we learn the existence of the prayers *Communicantes*, also *Hunc igitur* and *Quam oblationem*, lastly, the conclusion *Per quam hæc omnia*, which at Whitsunday preceded the Consecration of the honey and milk prepared for those about to be baptized. The *Diesque nostros*, which is known to have been added by Pope Gregory I., is here awanting; for when we find similar words in the Mass in *natali episcoporum* they do not belong to the regular Formel, but to an insertion peculiar to that festival. The present position of the Pax after the Canon, Pope Innocent I. records.

The old liturgical MSS. of the Gallican Rite which were previously known, were fully thrown into the shade by the eleven Gallican Masses which Franz Joseph Mone edited in 1850 from the Reichenan Palimpsest of the sixth century. They contain, likewise, merely the portions which vary, but which as we have already remarked are the most important parts of the Gallican Liturgy. We find here Prayers after the Lesson from the prophets, Collects (called in the Gallican Prefaces), Prayers before and after the reading of the

Diptychs and for the kiss of peace, Prefaces and Post-sanctus, or short sentences leading from the Sanctus to the Consecration. After the Consecration follows the varying *Post-secreta*, which contains a remembrance of the sufferings of Christ, the offering up of His Body and Blood, and the Invocation of the Holy Spirit, and then the Introduction and Appendage to the Paternoster, Post-communion, and Benediction. Still older than Mone's MS., appears to be a Milanese Palimpsest from which Angelo Mai has edited fragments of the Gallican Mass.[25] The Gallican Rite in the sixth century is likewise described in the liturgical work of St. Germanus of Paris.

The Alexandrian Rite we cannot, indeed, carry so far back on manuscript authority, as especially in the East liturgical MS. are rarely to be found; still the perfect agreement of the orthodox Greek Liturgy of St. Mark with the Monophysite Coptic Liturgy of St. Cyril, shows that the Alexandrian Rite must already have possessed its present form in the first half of the fifth century, before the separation of the Monophysites from the unity of the Church. The peculiar position of the Intercessory prayer, James of Edessa had already noticed in the seventh century.[26] Probst calls attention to the fact that certain passages of the Canon cited in an Armenian Council from a missal of St. Athanasius agree *verbatim* with the Liturgy of St. Mark.

---

[25] Script. Vett. nova Coll. iii. p. 247.
[26] Assemani, *Bibl. Orient.* 1. p. 484.

The East Syrian Liturgy of the apostles Adœus and Maris must, although we can now only point to it in the hands of the Nestorians, have been in use long before the outbreak of this heresy in these Eastern regions. For it not only does not contain a single trace of Nestorianism, but also many passages which point to a very high antiquity. For instance, it forbids any mention of the Eucharist in presence of the unbaptized, and directs the Deacon after the withdrawal of the Catechumens and Penitents to call out, "Those who do not receive *it* must go away." The Anaphora of Theodore and of Nestorius are throughout imitations of the Liturgy of the Apostles. The former betrays no Nestorian influence, but the latter must have been compiled quite in the beginning of the Nestorian controversy, as the sect had already Greek-speaking adherents in the Roman Empire; for it has at the Invocation of the Holy Spirit the addition "changing them through Thy Holy Spirit," which is found thus only in the two Constantinopolitan Liturgies, and from them transferred to the Armenian. The East Syrian Rite is further represented by a later Anaphora, to be mentioned afterwards, which is contained in a MS. of the sixth century. We must also not overlook the fact that the Nestorian office can be shown to have already possessed in the fifth century its present aspect in substance, still less can it be doubted that the same can be said in reference to the Liturgy.

The Liturgy of St. James must, on the same grounds

as that of St. Mark, have already existed in the first half of the fifth century, for the Greek text of the orthodox Greeks and the Syrian text of the Monophysite Jacobites agree very closely with each other, at least in the Anaphora, although the remaining part of the Liturgy has in time departed somewhat from each other, with the Greeks, Jacobites, and Maronites. That the Syrian text of the Liturgy of St. James in the seventh century was the same as the present, is apparent in the treatise by James of Edessa, to which we have already alluded. That the two Constantinopolitan Liturgies are rightly attributed to St. Basil and St. Chrysostom, appears not only from the testimony of the Deacon Petrus, who, in the year 512, names the Liturgy of St. Basil as almost universally used in the East, and makes a quotation from it, but also from the still earlier testimony of St. Proclus, who rightly states St. Basil and St. Chrysostom as having revised the Liturgy of St. James, and places the Clementine still farther back.

Although all the Liturgies referred to above differ so much from each other in single points, yet when placed against the Clementine Liturgy it is impossible to mistake a certain common type in them all. That characteristic impress lies in this, that the Eucharistic prayer of thanksgiving, which extends from the Preface to the Consecration, and contains in the Clementine Liturgy a very elaborate Praise and Thanksgiving for the creation and redemption of mankind, and culminates in thanksgiving for the Institution of the Holy Eucharist, in all the other Liturgies appears either much shorter, or is almost altogether absent. For while the Liturgies of Jerusalem, Constantinople, Alexandria, and Seleucia contain to a certain extent an abridgment from the long thanksgiving prayer of the Clementine, that in the East Syrian Anaphora of the sixth century is, in fact, equally elaborate; while the Roman Mass retains only in the Preface the general idea that praise and thanks are due to God, and brings the words of Institution by prefixing a part of the Intercessory prayer into connection with an entirely different conception. The Gallican Liturgy occupies a sort of middle position; for while the duty of giving thanks enters more or less into its Prefaces, it connects also the beginning of the Canon with the Sanctus, and then rapidly passes over to the words of Institution. Further, the bidding prayer and blessings before the dismissal of the Catechumens, Energumens, and Penitents is wanting in all the Liturgies, with the exception of the Clementine.

If, then, the Clementine Liturgy is in many respects more elaborate than the others, the latter, on the other hand, have much which we do not find in the former. All the others have preparatory prayers at the beginning of the Liturgy, to which, in the Eastern Liturgies, the Trisagion also belongs; in the Roman Mass only on Good Fridays and in the Prime; while the Clementine Liturgy begins at once with the Scripture lessons and the psalms. It knows nothing of any recitation of the Creeds, or of prayers that accompany the kiss of peace and the offertory. It also gives neither Rubrics nor forms of prayer for the breaking of the Bread, although these, as before remarked, unquestionably find place before the Communion in a simple manner. The most striking feature, however, is the want in the Clementine Liturgy of the Lord's Prayer, which is not only found in all other Liturgies between the Canon and Communion, but also is everywhere introduced and closed with the same words (Præceptis salutaribus and Libera Nos).

If, then, the Clementine Liturgy represents a type departing from all others, and these others, notwithstanding these differences with one another, can be regarded in contrast with the Clementine as a single modified rite, the question arises which of the two forms of the celebration of the Lord's Supper is the most ancient,—a question which we shall endeavour to answer in the next section.

§ 3. Superior Antiquity of the Clementine Liturgy.

As we find, from the fifth century to the present day in all parts of the Church, only the Liturgies enumerated in the five classes which are not Clementine in use, we are therefore obliged to assign a greater antiquity to the Clementine Liturgy unless we are to adopt the strange but widely-spread opinion that it is the arbitrary composition of some private individual. This view, however, will be refuted by the numerous arguments derived from the contents and form of the Clementine Liturgy, which demonstrates its greater antiquity in contrast with all the others. As this fact is at first sight almost self-evident from a candid comparison of the Liturgies, and as the admirable line of evidence which Probst has given is accessible to the reader, we shall confine ourselves here to a short exposition of the most important proofs.

As regards the characteristic difference, viz. the great shortness of the Eucharistic prayer in the other Liturgies, this can only be explained as merely an abbreviation of the longer form contained in the *Apostolical Constitutions*. Not only does St. Proclus distinctly state that the action taken by St. Basil and St. Chrysostom with regard to the Liturgies was one principally of abbreviation, by which he plainly indicates that the Apostolic Liturgy made known by Clemens was the undoubted original, but this abbreviation declares itself to be the result of the gradual development of the Church's cyclic festivals. For while in the first beginning of the Church the Church's year had little influence upon the Liturgy, and Lent and Easter alone specially appear as festivals in the regular course of the year, the different miraculous events obtained by degrees their yearly commemoration, and then it became a matter of necessity to represent fully the entire history of redemption in each service. This tendency is most apparent in the Roman Mass, which of the full Eucharistic prayer before the consecration has preserved merely the general thought that it was meet to render thanks to God, but then through varying sentences in the Preface and the *Communicantes* brings forward the special obligation to render thanks which the particular festival required.

The dismissal of the Catechumens, Energumens, and Penitents, which in the Clementine Liturgy is a prominent function, accompanied with prayers and blessings, is in the other Liturgies entirely awanting, or only implied in a few significant words of the Deacon, expresses quite as clearly the conditions of the first three Christian centuries as does this custom, being set aside through the gradual disappearance of the Catechumens and the modification of the Penitential discipline. James of Edessa abundantly shows most distinctly that this function was withdrawn at a later period from the celebration of the Lord's Supper.

What is wanting in the Clementine Liturgy also betrays its greater antiquity. It is the only Liturgy which has not already adopted into it the Nicene Creed. There are also awanting the introductory prayer, which had later so generally passed from the private preparation of the celebrant into the Liturgy itself. In the same way the prayers connected with the oblation, of which the *Apostolical Constitutions* know nothing, belong to the latest part of the Liturgy, as, for instance, in the Roman Mass, while during the entire Middle Ages almost every Church had in this its own peculiar form. The omission of any notice of the Lord's Prayer is in the highest degree striking, as also the *Fractio Hostiæ* and *Commixtio specierum*, which immediately follows upon it. Still the last proceedings were preceded by the second litany recited by the Deacon, while the omission of the Lord's Prayer in a Liturgy proceeding from the Apostles must remain an unsolved problem.

Much in the Clementine Liturgy betrays plainly its use at the time of an emperor who persecuted the Christians, such as the Prayer for those imprisoned on account of the name of Jesus, or condemned to labour in the mines; further, those for the enemies and persecutors of the Christian faith; lastly, the peculiar manner in which the emperor, the government, and the army are prayed for, that they might be more friendly disposed towards the Christians.

The Church organisation which we find in our document also imply the highest antiquity. The clergy are divided into Bishops, Priests, and Deacons, who also officiate as doorkeepers, and the servants to which the Lectors and Cantors belong; while the editor of the *Philosophumena*, towards the beginning of the third century, no longer designates the minor order as servants, but as clergy. It is true that in three passages the *Apostolical Constitutions* mention the Sub-deacons, but those must be regarded in comparison with other passages as additions made in the third century. Probst also, with reason, states that the Ascetics, whom St. Hippolytus already mentions under this technical designation as one of the Church orders, are here, except in a later addition to a rubric, either designated by a description or as Eunuchs. The collecta of the Deacon after the Canon knows of no other Saints than the Martyrs.

Even so the dogmatic terminology, which in its ancient looseness of expression contrasts so strongly with the theological exactness of the later Liturgies, points to an ante-Arian period. For later, such easily misunderstood expressions as, "We surrender ourselves to the only unbegotten God and His Christ," or "Thou hast before all time begotten Thy Son by Thine own will, power, and goodness," would have been avoided. Nothing can be a greater perversion than to draw from such expressions, which are even to be found in the orthodox Fathers of the first century, a charge of Arianism.

But not only do the contents, but likewise the arrangement and form of the Clementine Liturgy, show its high antiquity. No other is in its combination and all its separate parts so simple and so penetrating, and brought together in so harmonious and organic a manner. It contains equally a superficial principle, which, in the later, especially the Oriental Liturgies, is either adorned by fruitless elaboration and careful ornamentation, or frequently concealed and rendered unintelligible by a quantity of details.

So far as the diction is concerned, we find in the *Apostolical Constitutions* neither the severe, condensed, strong style, full of meaning, which the Roman Mass adopted, nor the majestically sublime but somewhat overloaded and yet conventionally verbose style of the later Oriental Liturgies. The language loses itself more in irrelevant elaboration without being confined to fixed ecclesiastical modes of expression. It equally attains, led by clearness and sentiment of an outspoken Christian self-consciousness, to what is truly conform to edification and fact. It is exactly this want of the conventional ecclesiastical style which has principally led to the extraordinary opinion that the Clementine Liturgy is the production of a private individual, without considering that such a fixed specifically ecclesiastical mode of expression could only by degrees have evolved itself in and from the Church life. If the later Oriental Liturgies remind us of the Byzantine pictures, so the Clementine Liturgy might well be compared with the pictures in the Catacombs in their naïve simplicity and their formal connection with profane models.

We are therefore brought to the conclusion that in comparison with all other Liturgies the Clementine represents a more ancient period of time. But as these other Liturgies possessed substantially their present form since the beginning of the fifth century, we cannot place the process of change by which the Christian Liturgy passed over from that older form to these later forms later than the fourth century. Exactly at this time we have authentic witnesses to the fact; for, besides the testimony we have already referred to of St. Proclus, there is a passage which has been rather overlooked of St. Basil, in which he states that the Church of Neo-Cæsarea had preserved this Liturgy unaltered as it had existed in the time of St. Gregory Thaumaturgus. "In this Church was neither a rubric, nor a word, nor a symbol added to that which he had left behind him; therefore in consequence of the antiquity of its arrangement much appears deficient because his successors in the government of the Church had accepted and added nothing of that which had been brought forward after his time."[27] From this it follows that in the period betwixt Gregory Thaumaturgus and Basil important changes in the Liturgy had taken place; and not only, as Proclus indicates, abbreviations, but likewise additions.

Moreover, these alterations are not made abruptly, so as to sever the ritual continuity, but much more gradually, almost unwillingly, to meet the requirements of the Church. This might be not only anticipated from the experience of the Catholic Church, but finds its documentary evidence in a primitive Syrian Anaphora,

[27] *De Spirito Sancto*, c. 29.

which is preserved in a MS. in the British Museum, of the sixth century, and so far as it is still legible has been published by us in a Latin translation.[23] This Anaphora, belonging to the East Syrian Rite, stands midway between the Clementine Liturgy and the others. Its Consecration prayer is neither so long as that in the former nor so short as those in the latter; for though it also omits the enumeration of the single acts of creation and the Old Testament history, it enlarges with even greater elaboration upon the being of God in Himself and the creation of man, while the later Liturgies comprise this also in few words. In one of the oldest of the Gallican Liturgies we find still greater abbreviation, but still entering more into some points; while the later Oriental Liturgies give the Consecration prayer from beginning to end only in outline, and the Romish Church has actually left out all from the beginning to the end. In the same way it is apparent from the Canons of the Synod of Laodicea and the Homilies of St. Chrysostom, that at that time, that is, at a time when the altering of the ritual had already begun, the prayers and blessings over the Catechumens and Penitents were still constantly in use.

There are still, however, two false conclusions, which might readily be drawn from what has gone before, which require refutation. It must not be supposed that prior to the Liturgical revision of the fourth century an

[23] G. Bickell, *Conspectus sic Syrorum literariæ*, pp. 71–73.

absolute sameness prevailed in the services of each Church. It is true that from that time there entered a marked and striking difference of individual Rites, inasmuch as in each separate ecclesiastical province what was naturally peculiar to each service was in different ways partly shortened and partly considerably added to ; but yet the germs, at least, of these local differences in the Eucharistic service were already present in the first three centuries, but were so completely overweighted by what was common to all, that it cannot unreasonably be said that during that early period there was but one Liturgy in the whole Church. In reference to Alexandria, Probst has accurately shown that both Clemens of Alexandria and Origen were even then acquainted with many expressions and prayers which in this form we only find in the Liturgy of St. Mark. The Clementine Liturgy, therefore, only on that account represents to us the Eucharistic service of the entire pre-Constantine Church, because the local differences were proportionally extremely small; but if we are to express ourselves correctly, we recognise it as the original type from which in the fourth century the Liturgy of St. James proceeded.

Further, we must guard ourselves against the position that we regard the Liturgy contained in the *Apostolical Constitutions* as unquestionably and in every particular proportional and apostolic. It is self-evident that we must make it the groundwork of our inquiry, because it is the only complete and connected document which makes us acquainted with the primitive Christian and apostolic Eucharistic service, and renders to us truly that service wholly and entire. We are, however, persuaded that, in particular, not only the then existing local peculiarities can be brought in touch with it, but our documents have also their entire singular properties, which must be justified by unanimous witness of the other Liturgies. As, then, in the comparison of the Christian and the Jewish rites we can employ the Clementine Liturgy as a representative of the former, we must here state beforehand on what occasions and on what grounds we forsake its authority and apply ourselves to other services.

Then we have simply to accept the fact that the collects twice recited by the Deacon—once before the Preface, and again after the Canon—and the Intercessory prayer of the Priest after the Consecration on each occasion contains the same petitions; and that a difference between them exists only in so far that the last collect, in accordance with its object, must be somewhat shorter, that these collects were simple bidding prayers, while the Intercessory prayer was the application of the Eucharistic offering. We must, however, regard it as something accidental and arbitrary when on the one occasion persons or petitioners are mentioned of whom on another there is no mention. We must, for instance, in the opening collect of the *Apostolical Constitutions* enlarge from the two other Formularies the Prayer for emperor and government, the Commemoration of the Saints and departed believers, as well as the prayer for a good harvest; and, on the other hand, transfer from the former to the latter the memento for givers of alms and oblations. But that we have the fullest right to those enlargements can be shown from the *Apostolical Constitutions* themselves; for in the short description they give of the first collect in the second book, cap. 57, they mention distinctly that the Deacon offers up prayers for the emperor and the worldly authorities. The omission of this in the corresponding part of the Liturgy, in the eighth book, is therefore quite accidental, and nothing more than a singular incompleteness in the text.

It is further certain that this threefold bidding prayer is merely a threefold repetition of one and the same order of prayer which, as we shall afterwards see, had its original place in the Pre-communion; but was afterwards, from the beginning of the Christian Church, repeated by the Priest after the Consecration, to make prominent the conception, that through the Eucharistic offering the health-bringing operation of the passion of Christ was conferred upon man. The two positions of the prayer stand in an ever-varying relation to each other. The same supplications which the believing people bring before God as a Prayer-offering are repeated in the Canon as an Oblation prayer, and obtain, through their union with the only full acceptable offering to God, the certainty of their being heard. There is immediately connected with it a continued repetition of the same supplication, partly in order to ensure the participation of the people with the Intercessory prayer of the Priest, partly to occupy the silence during the Breaking of Bread. This original identity of the three bidding prayers, which is expressed externally by the second, beginning with the word " again," and the third with the words " again and always," oblige us to conclude that the supplication following upon each in all three prayers must have been originally the same. With greatest truth have the collects, and especially from the omissions of the first the second has preserved the right order. On the other hand, the Intercessory prayer in the *Apostolical Constitutions* has come, from the same cause, somewhat into confusion, as it places the prayer for the laity after those for the rulers and for the dead. The right order can be readily restored from the collects in the *Apostolical Constitutions* and from the original Intercessory prayer preserved in the Liturgy of St. James, namely, the Syrian and its followers. A closer consideration of the single supplications can naturally only be brought out after a comparison with the Jewish expressions.

While we have hitherto been enabled to place the Liturgy of the *Apostolical Constitutions*, from internal evidence, in its right position, the evidence derived from the other Liturgies enables us also to point out two necessary corrections in the Preface. First, we cannot hold the division of the Consecration prayer in the

Clementine Liturgy, according to which the praise of the Divine Being, the thanks for the creation, and for the Old Testament plan of salvation, is placed in the Preface before the Sanctus; but the thanks for the redemption through Christ is placed in the Canon, notwithstanding its high antiquity, for the original order. But, on the other hand, we must prefer the order contained in the old East Syrian Anaphora, which has the entire Consecration prayer after the Sanctus in the Canon; and merely states in the Preface the general idea that it is meet and the duty of believers, along with the angels, to give God praise and thanks, while the whole presumption for this thought is appropriate in the Canon. The later Liturgies have, in fact, no longer a full Consecration prayer. One must, however, admit that the Alexandrian, Old Gallican, and probably also Nestorian Liturgies connect themselves with the Clementine; while the Liturgy of St. James follows that Old East Syrian Anaphora which commends itself as original from its greater simplicity.

On the other hand, the Clementine Liturgy departs from all others as regards the Sanctus sung by the people after the Preface, with the exception, perhaps, of the Alexandrian. For while in all others the words of the Sanctus are the same with those in the Roman Mass, it consists in the Clementine Liturgy only of the seraphic hymn (Holy, holy, holy is the Lord of Sabaoth, Heaven and earth are full of His glory), which close with the 26th verse of Ps. cxviii., " Blessed for ever and ever, Amen." On the other hand, we find the omitted words in another part of this Liturgy. The answer of the people to the words, "Holy things for the holy," consists of the close and beginning of our *Gloria in excelsis*, but it is followed by the sentence taken from Ps. cxviii. 25-27, "Hosanna to the Son of David. Blessed is He that cometh in the name of the Lord, God, the Lord: and He has appeared to us. Hosanna in the highest." All these words, seeing that they are taken from one and the same passage in the psalm, had probably originally stood after the Sanctus, for the words, "Hosanna to the Son of David," are to be found still in the Sanctus of the East Syrian and Mozarabic Liturgies; and although the words, "God, the Lord, and He has appeared to us," are now nowhere apparent, yet it is amply included through the common origin from which it springs. These passages from the psalms in the oldest Liturgy seem to have been greatly loved, and to have been suitable to different places, for they are equally to be found at the end of a primitive prayer after the Consecration which has been preserved in the seventh book of the *Apostolical Constitutions*, cap. 26. The significance, likewise, of these corrections in the Preface can only receive their full elucidation by the later comparison with the Jewish rites.

That the Breaking of the Host, although not specially mentioned, must have existed in the Clementine Eucharistic service, and is even implied, has been already noticed. As to the more complicated question regarding the Lord's Prayer we shall not enter upon it at present, as it is hardly a necessity for the course of our inquiry.

On the other hand, it will not be out of place to take this opportunity to consider the singular proposition, that the primitive Christian Eucharistic service consisted wholly of the Lord's Prayer, which has been frequently maintained by Protestant authors, and by Catholics (naturally under reservation of the words of Institution) most unaccountably accepted; while, on the contrary, the greatest doubts have been raised as to the original existence of the Lord's Prayer in the Eucharistic service. The Invocation on the assertion of St. Justin, that the elements were consecrated by "words of prayer proceeding from Christ," is almost entirely given up, and could only be raised by those who are acquainted with Justin only through quotations, for this holy martyr repeats distinctly the words of Institution, and indicates the Consecration as the effect of the recitation of them. There remains then only the well-known passage of St. Gregory the Great; those however, who are of the firm persuasion with us that this great and holy pope could think logically and express himself after the manner of a reasonable man, must agree with Probst's declaration, that Gregory in the first part of his passage justifies the exclusion of the Lord's Prayer from the Canon by the example of the Apostles, but in the second part defends the insertion of this prayer in that part which follows the Canon on grounds of propriety against those who would entirely exclude it.

§ 4. THE CLEMENTINE LITURGY IN USE DURING THE FIRST THREE CENTURIES.

It has already been sufficiently shown that the Clementine Liturgy surpasses all the others in antiquity, and was in use in the Church before the fourth century. There remains then only the proof that the Christian writers of all lands during the first three centuries as far back as the apostolic age, invariably treat of the Eucharistic service in such a manner as in substance exactly corresponds with the Clementine. From this it will follow that this Liturgy was completed by the apostles, and during the entire ante-Nicene period was used in all the churches, as the liturgic differences of single apostolic churches was too insignificant that there could be any talk on that account of different Liturgies.

In conducting this proof, which shall almost entirely follow, Probst, who with extraordinary acuteness has shown from the allusions of the ante-Nicene Fathers of the Church on the old Liturgy, as well as from passages in which hitherto writers have found only the most general and indefinite ideas, has worked out the most detailed and decided conclusions as to the old Christian Eucharistic service. As, therefore, what follows is substantially a general glance at the connection of the most impartial of Probst's conclusions, we must refer to Probst for a clearer exposition of these grounds, and shall only quote from the Fathers when we have to add something to the materials brought together by that learned man.

The proof given by Probst is the more surprising, as during the first three centuries the prohibition to allow anything relative to the Eucharistic celebration to come to the knowledge of the unbaptized was strictly observed. With very few exceptions the Fathers of the Church during this period present only quite hidden allusions to the Eucharistic service. Still it would be going too far to deny the existence of written Liturgies during this period, as founding upon a misunderstood passage of St. Basil, taken from its context, on the authority of the Liturgy existing in no Biblical work, the tradition of the Church is to be regarded as of equal authority with the Holy Scriptures. On the other hand, Probst shows well that St. Justin, Origen, Novatian and other Fathers contain distinct quotations from the liturgic prayers, which have previously their written fixed form.

St. Cyprian mentions, as does the still older Commodian, the exclamation *Sursum corda*, and the response *Habemus ad Dominum*. Origen describes in one place pointedly the whole service, in another only the Canon, and notices the prayers and blessings over the Catechumens, Energumens, and Penitents, the prayers of the faithful before the Offertorium, the Preface consisting of praise and thanksgiving, the Sanctus, then passing over the Consecration, the Exomologesis (the confession of sinfulness and the prayer to be freed from it through the divine sacrament which follows the Invocation of the Holy Spirit), the Intercessory prayer for living and dead, the doxologic conclusion of the Canon, the chanting of the thirty-third Psalm during the Communion; lastly, the thanksgiving prayer which follows it. From these facts it follows that the Liturgy of Origen corresponds in general with the Clementine, although several peculiarities of the later Liturgy of St. Mark can be found in him.

The teacher of Origen, Clemens of Alexandria, carries on the long Eucharistic prayer with the Sanctus almost *verbatim* according to the Clementine Liturgy; but that these and many similar passages of the most ancient Fathers in which a *verbatim* agreement with the Consecration prayer of the *Apostolical Constitutions* as to the being of God in Himself, the creation, the Old Testament history, and the redemption through Christ is mentioned, are actually taken from the Liturgy, is proved by the distinct testimony of St. Athenagoras.

To St. Hippolytus are ascribed by the Copts and the Æthiopians thirty-eight Canons, the Arabic text of which has been published by Haneberg.[29] The contents of this text agree in the main with the Greek, in part with the

[29] *Canones St. Hippolyti Arabice*, Munich 1870.

apostles' decrees distinctly ascribed to Hippolytus.[30] Its contents, and in a great degree even its verbal expressions, correspond with the eighth book of the *Apostolical Constitutions*. These decrees found reception in an older Clementine Octateuch which is different from the *Apostolical Constitutions* but unfortunately only preserved in fragments in the Syrian text,[31] at first giving teachings and ordinances of Christ, then shorter expressions of a single apostle in Greek,[32] which are cited by Clemens of Alexandria as Holy Scripture, and to a great extent correspond with the seventh book of the *Apostolical Constitutions*, and also contains the substantial contents of the eighth book; and lastly, the well-known Apostolical Canons. In the Coptic and Æthiopic recensions [33] the first is wanting, the so-called book containing the Testament of Jesus Christ; instead of that, those proverbs of a single apostle form the commencement. On these follow, then, the foregoing in the Syrian text and the ecclesiastical ordinances referred to Christ Himself, which touch upon the same points as

---

[30] There is first "the apostolic teaching about the Charismata" which Hippolytus and other sources have pointed out, and which now form the beginning of the eighth book of the *Constitutions*. Then "the apostolic regulations regarding ordination by Hippolytus," with which probably the canonical regulations of St. Paul and the apostles Peter and Paul may be combined.

[31] Published by Lagarde, *Religiose juris Ecclesiasticæ antiquissimæ Syriace*, pp. 2-61.

[32] First published by my father, W. Bickell, *Geschichte des Kirchen Rechts*, i. p. 107.

[33] Comp. Tatian, *The Apostolical Constitutions in Coptic*, London 1805; Lagarde, *Religiose*, pp. 11-16; Rudolf, *Ad Hist. Æthæope com.* 305.

those which follow, and show a correspondence with the eighth book of the *Constitutions*, so that striking repetitions of the same themes in the *Apostolical Constitutions* were already to be found in the older Clementine Octateuch. Our present collection of *Apostolical Constitutions* in eight books, which is the latest textual form of this whole literature, was preceded by an older recension in the Syrian, Arabic, and Æthiopic languages, which only contained the first six books. The Syrian text published by Lagarde [34] characterises itself by its entire freedom from the numerous later interpolations. Thus there is wanting in it the description of the Liturgy in the second book, while it describes the quarto-deciman Eastern festival told us by Epiphanius; there is also here to be noticed a primitive Syrian collection of Canons, " the teaching of the Apostles," which Cureton [35] has published from a MS. of the sixth century. In the later Parisian MS., from which Lagarde had earlier published them, they are falsely called (as also by Barhebræus) " the teaching of Adæus," because they generally followed that old and probably genuine history; besides that, they come here by mistake between the extracts from the older Clementine Octateuch with which they originally stood in no connection.

Of this whole literature which we have been obliged to describe somewhat fully on account of the confused

---

[34] *Dedæcalia Apostolorem Syrian Liturgy*, 1854.
[35] *Ancient Syrian Documents*, pp. 24-35.

relation of the different texts to each other, the Arabic Canon of Hippolytus unquestionably bears the character of the greatest antiquity, and must at all events, if not by Hippolytus himself, at least have been completed in his time. It is therefore a matter of interest to compare their sketch with the Liturgy. They connect, just as the eighth book of the *Apostolical Constitutions* does, the description of the Eucharistic celebration with the Consecration of the bishop, only the description is a good deal shorter.[36] The Oblation is mentioned, and then the responsory before the Preface ("The grace of the Lord, etc., be with you all;" "and with thy spirit." "Lift up your hearts;" "We lift them up unto the Lord." "Let us give thanks to the Lord;" "It is meet and right"). In the description of the offering, Baptism (Canon 19), the prayer of the faithful in the ante-communion, and the distribution of the communion, with the words, "This is the Body of Christ," and "This is the Blood of Christ," upon which the response of Amen follows, are spoken of. Further, there is mentioned the white robes of the clergy, the Scripture lessons by the Lector at the beginning of the Mass, the fans of the Deacons, and the Mass for the dead, which ought not to be held on Sunday. (Canons 39, 29, 33.)

---

[36] The Greek "Apostolic ordinances regarding ordination" of Hippolytus betray at this place nothing as to the Liturgy. The two Coptic texts of the older Clementine Octateuch give a short but more rubrical representation, which looks like an extract from the Liturgy in the eighth book of the *Apostolical Constitutions*. The Æthiopic text is fuller, but connects itself with the specific Æthiopic rite.

As the later pseudo-apostolic collection related to the Hippolytus Canons still belong at least to the ante-Nicene period, and are not without value for our immediate object, the mention of some liturgical points noticed in it will not be out of place. In the Syrian text of the Clementine Octateuch the known call of the Deacon, "Let us stand properly" (Στῶμεν καλῶς), though not accidentally brought out in the *Apostolical Constitutions*, is mentioned and indicated as properly the beginning of the celebration, after which no one was permitted to enter the church. Probably it preceded the call to the collect prayer, for it is named in contrast to the solemn offering as the thanksgiving (Canon), during which equally no late comer was permitted to enter. The Deacon then ought equally to exhort those standing idly before the door by brotherly remonstrance and wholesome shame to greater zeal, either at the oblation, or at the first collect, or at the thanksgiving, also at the second collect at the end of the Canon; a new proof that the repetition of the collect after the Intercessory prayer is original, and no interpolation.

In the "teaching of the Apostles," falsely called the teaching of Adæus, the position during prayer is towards the east, the singing of psalms in the Liturgy, the standing up at the Gospel, the celebration of Epiphany, Lent, Good Friday, Easter, the Ascension, and Whitsunday, as well as the Commemoration of the Martyrs and other dead, are directed.

After this episode, rendered necessary by the records

ascribed to St. Hippolytus, we turn now to his teacher, St. Irenæus, and confine ourselves to a short statement of one of Probst's most important results. In one of the fragments discovered by Maffei, Irenæus expresses the Invocation of the Holy Spirit word for word as we find it in the Clementine Liturgy.[37]

For the first half of the second century St. Justin gives us his testimony, the only ante-Nicene Father of the Church who gives us a connected description of the Eucharistic service. Although this owes its origin, not to a liturgical, but to an apologetic interest, still Probst could with the help of scattered notices in other parts of his writings present us with the following picture of the Liturgy in use at that time. After the lessons from the prophets and the Gospels, the President held an exhortative discourse on what had been read. Then prayers were put up for the Catechumens among others. Then followed the prayers of the faithful for all mankind, responded to with the Kyrie Eleison. Then the kiss of peace, the bringing of bread and wine and water to the President, who received these oblations and delivered a long and solemn thanksgiving over them. In this thanksgiving, reference was made, not only to the sufferings of Christ, but God was also thanked for the creation and the redemption. What St. Justin gives us out of this prayer agrees exactly with the Clementine Liturgy. So he mentions the resurrection

---

[37] [This fragment is now generally considered as falsely attributed to Irenæus.—ED.]

immediately after the creation, which can only be explained by a comparison with the Clementine Preface. In this prayer a repetition of the words of intercessory prayer was connected. At the doxologic conclusion of the Canon, the people answered Amen. Deacons gave the faithful the consecrated elements. The agreement of this Liturgy with the Clementine is unmistakable.

The same thing is also true with regard to the liturgic references which towards the end of the first century are found in the Epistle of St. Clement of Rome to the Corinthians. It mentions a prayer for the Penitent which is strikingly like that in the *Apostolical Constitutions*. His proof for the saying that God is a God of peace, is taken almost *verbatim* from that Liturgy. He also refers to the resurrection after he had described the creation. What he says about the Old Testament history and the redemption through Christ comes from the same source. He even plays with the Sanctus in the following words: "With the myriads of angels who cry, 'Holy, holy, holy,' let us also assembled in church with one accord cry out, that we may participate in the wonderful gift of God, which no eye has seen, nor ear heard; for we shall find Jesus Christ our Saviour to be the High Priest of our offering."

From the New Testament itself we can so far only gather with absolute certainty that the words of Institution formed a substantial and unalterable part of the service, and that the bread was broken before the Communion. Other parts, as the kiss of peace and the prayer for all mankind, are indeed noticed, but without any distinct relation with the Liturgy. Probst has, with remarkable acuteness, endeavoured to find the entire contents of the Eucharistic thanksgiving prayer of the *Apostolical Constitutions* in the Epistles of St. Paul; but his deduction rests upon so many not very provable presumptions, that we can hardly expect a recognition of them from a dogmatic opposing side. In the meantime, we find ourselves in the agreeable position of dispensing with any such recognition, as the apostolical origin of our Liturgy rests upon a much more certain and unassailable basis, namely, on its agreement with Jewish rites and with the celebration of the Passover supper. Before, however, we can bring forward the proof of this, the Jewish Passover ritual, as well as the Sabbath morning service which lies at the root of the Pre-communion, must be presented; and it must be shown that its present substantial contents has been already in use at the time of the institution of the holy Eucharist.

II.

THE JEWISH RITUAL WHICH GAVE RISE TO THE OLD CHRISTIAN LITURGY.

§ 1. THE RITUAL OF THE PASSOVER SUPPER.

THE Book of the Mosaic Law contains, indeed, the divine command that every Israelitish family must on the evening of 14th Nisan feed on the undivided and unbroken roasted paschal lamb with unleavened bread and bitter herbs, in remembrance of the freedom of the chosen people from the Egyptian bondage, but prescribes little as to the mode of the celebration; and that little, even according to the testimony of the Jewish revelation, is mainly confined to the first Passover celebrated in Egypt, as appears from the preparation at the supper for the journey, and the sprinkling the threshold and door-posts with the blood of the lamb.

On the other hand, the later Jewish literature makes us acquainted with a rich and complicated Passover ritual, which we must proceed to describe from these sources, and to show that it was then, as it is at present, already in use at the time of the Institution of the holy Eucharist, before we can lay down its agreement with the old Christian Liturgy.

The oldest source is the Mischna, which is known to have received its present form from Rabbi Juda Hakkadosch towards the end of the second century after Christ, but consists of accounts of older controversies, mostly belonging to teachers during the previous three centuries. It contains a pretty full description of the Passover ritual, to which we must again refer later on. The Tosiphtha gives us an important addition to it, which contains the collected additions to the Mischna by Rabbi Juda's scholars. The discussions which took place after the close of the Mischna by living teachers on its fixed materials are, as is known, contained in the two Gemaras, that of Jerusalem, which received in substance its present form in the fourth, and that of Babylon, towards the end of the fifth centuries. Unfortunately, both Gemaras afford little help for our object; as the Jerusalem Gemara comments very shortly upon that section of the Mischna, and the Babylonian hardly enters upon the ritual, but is engaged on discussions of a totally different kind.

During the centuries which followed the close of the Talmud the literary activity of the Jews was not great; and if it again increased during the Geonaisch period, still the ritualistic and Talmud exegetic writings of Saadias, Gaon Hai, Amram, and others, which are here and there quoted in the later collection, are works no longer preserved. On the other hand, the catena of authorities is after the eleventh century no longer interrupted;

and we may now confine ourselves merely to notice the most important as the explainers of the Talmud, Rabbi Isaac Ben Jacob of Fez (1103), Rabbi Solomon Ben Isaac, called Raschi (1105), who compiled a commentary on several of the Talmudic treatises, and among them that on the Easter Festival, whose grandson, Rabbi Samuel Ben Meir, although he commented merely on the treatises left by his grandfather, yet made an exception exactly with the last chapter of the Easter treatise, in which the Passover ritual is described; further, the celebrated philosopher, Moses Maimonides, in his *Talmudic Encyclopœdia*, and, lastly, Jacob Bar Ascher (1340), in the first volume of his *Arba Turim*, a compilation of the whole Jewish law and ceremonial, which formed the groundwork of the similar collected works, in sixteenth century, of Joseph Caro, *Scholchan Aruch*.

The ritual of the Passover evening itself, contained in MSS. of the so-called *Oster Haggada* since the tenth century, affords us the most direct testimony for the existence of those interesting usages. By this name, which comes next to the account given to the children before the supper of the exodus from Egypt, the entire celebration of Passover evening is also designated. In reliance on these authentic directories, but still keeping in view the varying sketches in the Talmudic and Rabbinic writings, we shall endeavour to give a clear representation of the Jewish celebration of the Passover. If we appear frequently to enter too much into detail, this may be forgiven us, as many apparently-irrelevant minutiæ may be found later in the composition of the Christian Liturgy to have more importance.

The Paschal lamb was an actual offering. It was slain in the temple, its blood was sprinkled by the priest on the altar, its fatty parts were burnt on the altar, its flesh was consumed as a sacrificial meal. Therefore, after the destruction of Jerusalem, when the temple service, with its priests and sacrifices, came to an end, it could no longer be eaten. The same thing is true of the Chagiga, the meat of a slain thank-offering, which was wont to be previously brought with the Passover supper. There were thus several differences between the Passover celebration as it was conducted after the second destruction of the temple, and that in the earlier period, which must each time be carefully noticed.

We must still premise some general observations on the Jewish ritual. The so-called Benedictions are quite short, after a specific form founded on the Schema, which accord generally with our "good intention," and have the purpose to give all proceedings, enjoyments, and all joyful as well as painful events a relation to the power and will of God, and to recognise His power and goodness in them. For example, the Benediction before drinking wine, "Blessed be Thou, the Lord our God, King of the world, that Thou hast created the fruit of the vine." If the proceeding is one prescribed by the Law, then this is specially mentioned in the formula.

This, for instance, is the blessing in washing the hands, "Praised be Thou, the Lord our God, King of the world, that Thou hast sanctified us by Thy command, and commanded us to wash the hands." There are, however, also Benedictions which contain a complete praising of God or a thanksgiving or prayer. In each case there is at the close a short clause added, beginning with, "Praised be Thou, O Lord." When, however, the Benediction begins with "Praised be Thou," it is termed a long, and not a short one. For instance, take here the blessing which is said at the end of the chanting of the Psalms, "Thy name be glorified for ever, O our King, God great and holy, King in heaven and on earth; for there is due from us, O Lord our God and God our Father, song and praise, fame and song, power and dominion, triumph, greatness and glory, praise and glory, holiness and kingdom, blessing and acknowledgment, from henceforth and for ever. Praised be Thou, O Lord, God, King, great, through praises, God of thanksgiving, Lord of miracles, that Thou pleasest to accept the hymns of song, King, God, living for ever." The notice in the Mischna that the clause of the Benedictions in the temple have at the beginning always ended with "from everlasting," is of peculiar interest for the comparison with the Christian prayers; later however, against those who denied the immortality, the words "to everlasting" were added. Amen was responded to every blessing.

The ritual eating of the different Paschal meats was

always accompanied by a blessing, and it was necessary to eat at least as much as the size of an olive, while of each of the four ritual wine-cups at least more than half must be drank. These four cups must also be mixed with water. At the Passover supper it was not necessary that the partakers should be, as in the first Passover celebrated in Egypt, prepared for a journey; but they reclined at the table, leaning on the left side, in order to symbolise their freedom from Egyptian slavery, as only freemen and nobles eat in this position.

This position, moreover, was strictly prescribed for the drinking of the four cups and the first symbolic eating of the unleavened bread.

The Passover supper begins, as on other festivals, with the Kiddusch or Consecration of the festival. This consists in this that after the first cup is filled for each participant, and the usual blessing of the wine said over it, the Kiddusch Benediction is prayed, in which God is thanked for the sending of these holy times, and especially for the Passover festival; and another is prayed, which thanks God that those present have been preserved in life to this day. Then the first cup is drank. If the 14th Nisan is a Friday, the first three verses of the second chapter of Genesis is recited before the blessing of the wine, and the Kiddusch inserts in several places the mention of the Sabbath. If it is a Saturday, then, after the Kiddusch, the blessing upon the light as well as the Habdala benediction, which at the end of the Sabbath inserts thanks for the distinction between holy and profane days.

After a first washing of the hands, at which, at least according to the common practice, the usual blessing is omitted, there was brought at the time of the temple the roasted Passover Lamb, with the Chagiga meat, the unleavened bread, bitter herbs, and other green herbs; the Charoseth, a sweet fruit sauce; and lastly, a vessel with vinegar or salt water, which, however, is not mentioned by Maimonides. At present these articles of food are placed on the tables at the blessing, in remembrance of the Passover, and to the Chagiga it is customary to add two boiled dishes, at present generally an egg and a bone with some meat upon it. The number of cakes of unleavened bread required for the ceremony is at present three, but, according to Maimonides, two were considered enough at the time of the temple.

In order now to show that the supper was to begin, the housefather or president takes one of the green herbs, dips it in the salt water (according to Maimonides in the *Charoseth*), says the blessing over the fruits of the earth, eats then of the herbs, and hands it to the others present. At present the middle of the three cakes is broken, and one-half preserved in order at the end of the supper to serve as the last thing to be eaten in remembrance of the Passover lamb, with a piece of which the supper was formerly concluded. This preserved piece is called Asikoman or the supper. It is self-evident that the Asikoman only became customary after the destruction of the temple, as it was a substitute for the Passover lamb no longer present. Maimonides is aware of it, but places the breaking of the bread, not at this part of the ceremony, but later, before the blessing of the bread, and gives this breaking no practical bearing upon the Asikoman, but a symbolical one in as far as that bread should represent the bread of poverty and misery.

The president raises the unleavened bread and says, in the Chaldaic language, "This is the bread of history which our fathers have eaten in the land of Egypt. Each hungry one come and eat, each necessitous one come and hold the Passover." Later, there was added to this, "This year here, next year in the Land of Israel; this year servants, next year free."

The table (later only the dishes with the bread) was now removed from the place of the president, and the second cup was mixed. The youngest present then asked, "Why is this night different from all other nights? For all other nights we eat leavened and unleavened bread, but in this only unleavened bread. In all other nights we eat other herbs; in this night only bitter: in all other nights we eat roasted, stewed, and boiled meat; in this night only roasted: in all other nights we do not require once to dip it; in this night we must twice: in all other nights we eat sometimes reclining and sometimes sitting; in this night only reclining." This question, so far as it regarded the roasted meat offering, was naturally omitted after the destruction of the temple.

The president then related the so-called Eastern Haggada, in which he informed his son, or whoever had put the question regarding the occasion of the festival. This custom was based upon several passages of the Mosaic law, when the fathers were bound to explain to their children the meaning of the Passover ceremonies (Ex. xii. 26, xiii. 8; Deut. vi. 20). The Haggada begins with a short narrative of the wonderful freedom from Egypt, and of the duty to narrate thankfully this divine act of goodness, viz. in the Passover night, based upon Deut. vi. 21. After some remarks on the varied states of the heart of the inquirers, which were indicated in the four relative passages of the Thora and on the time of the before-written instruction, it begins with a reference to the idolatry of the predecessors of Abraham, the Covenant of God with the patriarchs, and salvation of the Israelic people from their oppressors. There is connected with this a full exhortation following the text, word for word, of the twenty-sixth chapter of Deuteronomy, vers. 5–9; in closing this, there is then narrated at length the plagues and punishment of the Egyptians, while the notice of each plague is accompanied with dipping the fingers in the wine. In contrast with this, the benefits which God hath bestowed on the Israelites are brought forward.

After the table is again replaced before him, the housefather explains the significance of the Passover

Lamb (a notice which was later changed from an account to a mere reference), of the unleavened bread, and the bitter herbs, when each time the relative objects are raised on high. Then he adds, " In each generation each one must so regard himself as if he himself were led out of Egypt, as it is written ; and on that account what the Lord, by my exodus from Egypt, has done for me. Not only has the holy One, the high praised One freed our fathers, but us also with them, as it is written. He has brought us out from thence in order to bring us into the land which He promised to our fathers in order to give it to us ; " the cup is then held on high, when he proceeds, " Therefore are we bound to thank, to praise, to worship, to declare, to magnify, to glorify, to bless, to raise, and celebrate Him who has done all these things for our fathers and for us ; He has brought us out of servitude to freedom, out of grief to joy, out of mourning to festival, out of darkness to great light, and out of subjection to emancipation ; therefore, let us sing before Him a new song. Hallelujah." There follows then the first part of the Hallel, consisting of 113th and 114th Psalms ; a Benediction which gives thanks for the freedom from Egypt, prays for the restoration of the sacrificial worship, and closes with the sentence, " Praised be Thou, O Lord, that Thou hast freed Israel ; " lastly, the blessing of the wine, after that the second cup is drank.

The actual supper now begins, which previously commenced only in appearance and was interrupted by the Haggada. After a second washing of the hands, accompanied by the usual blessing, the president takes one of the cakes, breaks it (thus according to Maimonides, while now, as already noticed, the breaking takes place before the Haggada), lays the broken cake under a whole cake, raises both on high, recites over it the usual blessing of the bread, to which he adds another over the command to eat unleavened bread, upon which he eats of both cakes and gives it to the others.[38] The bitter herb is then dipped in the Charoseth, and is partaken of in the same manner after the blessing on the command to eat bitter herbs is recited. According to Maimonides, the blessing on the command to eat unleavened bread and bitter herbs can be combined in one blessing, and both eaten together. It is now the custom to take the third and undermost cake, dip it with bitter herb in the Charoseth, and without a blessing to partake of it. This is done in remembrance of the temple and of the Paschal lamb, for Hillel had the custom to eat a portion of the lamb along with bread and bitter herbs, in order, literally, to fulfil the command, "Ye shall eat the flesh with unleavened bread and bitter herbs." From the object of this ceremony it follows that it was

---

[38] As the broken bread has a symbolic meaning, a portion of both cakes lying under each other, the whole one and the broken one. Before the destruction of the temple both halves of the broken cake lay under the whole one, now only one-half did, the other half is put aside in order to use it later at the close of the supper, instead of the last morsel of the lamb.

first adopted after the destruction of the temple, as Maimonides, indeed, distinctly asserts. In the time of the temple, therefore, only two, and not three, cakes were used.

The ritual eating of the Chagiga and the Passover lamb, along with the blessings which preceded them, obviously ceased with the cessation of the sacrificial worship.

The actual supper which followed is connected with no further ceremonial, and the wine which was drank during it was not reckoned as belonging to the four ritual Passover cups. It was only at the last morsel that a piece of the Paschal lamb was eaten, its place being taken later by the Asikoman, or the half of the broken cake which was laid aside.

After the conclusion of the supper the third cup was mixed, and the usual table blessing, the thanksgiving after the meal, was said over it. It begins with an Antiphonal thanksgiving to God between the president and the company at table; then follow the Benedictions, which give thanks for the food and all the other divine benefits. The expressions in these two are, "Praised be Thou, O Lord, who nourishes all," and "Praised be Thou, O Lord, for the land and the food." Then follows a prayer for the people of Israel, for Jerusalem, Zion, the house of David, and the Temple, to which on the Sabbath a prayer appropriate to the day closes it. The prayer which follows prays the God of the people of Israel, of their fathers, of the Messiah, and the Holy

City, to think favourably, and accord mercy and help. In this prayer mention of the Passover festival is inserted. The clause, "Praised be Thou, O Lord, that in Thy mercy rebuilt Jerusalem, Amen," is found in the Portuguese-Jewish ritual before the Sabbath prayer. Then follows a longer prayer, which gives praise and thanks to God for help already given, but consists further of a succession of short petitions. They all begin with the words, "The merciful One, may He," and are somewhat different in the German and the Portuguese rituals. The first petition relates, in both rituals, to the honour and glory of God. Those which follow pray for blessing on the people of Israel, for their freedom from their oppressors, for the coming of the Messianic time, and eternal life. At several places there is the response, "Amen;" and on the Sabbath an appropriate petition is inserted. In the German ritual, the last of these petitions is for peace. The table-blessing closes with several appropriate passages of the Holy Scripture on the bounty of God towards those who honour Him, and the wine-blessing, after which the third cup is drank.

After a few biblical petitions to God for the punishment of the heathen are sent forth at the open doors, the fourth cup is mixed and the second part of the Hallel Psalms, 115 to 118, is recited over it. To the first four verses of Psalm 118 those present respond with the words, "For His mercy endureth for ever," while the Cantor only chants the first half of the verse as the Midrasch on the Psalms points out. In this Midrasch it is said that three must be present during the recitation of the Hallel, because one must first pray the words, "Praise the Lord," etc., and the two others must respond to him. From the Tosiphtha, in the last chapter of the treatise *Pesachim*, we learn further that in verse 26 of the same psalm a double response is necessary to the first half of the verse, the words, " In name of the Lord" are responded; in the second, the words, "Out of the house of the Lord." The whole passage reads thus : " If the president allows others to recite the Hallel, they must go to him, not he to them. Whoever allows the Hallel to be recited by his young sons and daughters, he must respond along with them at those passages which are responded to. At which passages must he then respond? Answer, when they come to the words, 'Blessed is He that cometh,' he must say with them, 'In the name of the Lord.' Also after the words, 'We bless you,' he must say with them, 'Out of the house of the Lord.'" It seems almost as if these oldest sources knew of no responses except at this verse. Still, it is certain that there were responses in the first four verses, also in verse 25, as is self-apparent. In the last passage, that is, at each half verse, one of the company repeats first the "O Lord, Hosanna," and then the "O Lord, send now prosperity." The present custom is this, that from verse 21 to the end of the psalm the whole verse is twice said, with the exception of verse 25, in which the company respond by repeating each half verse. On the other hand, at verse 26 the old mode of recitation, as pointed out in the Tosiphtha, is given up, and it is treated in the same way as the other closing verses. The oldest authority for the repetition of the closing verse of the Hallel appears to be in the Babylonian Gemara, where it is said, "Where it is the custom to repeat the Hallel, let it be done, where it is simply said it may be let alone." Still it must be remarked that in some communities where the half verse is not repeated, Hallelujah is added to it, as an Arabic MS., noticed by Neubauer in the *Grätzschen Monatschrift* for July 1871, does.

There was generally added to the Hallel the following Benediction, or, more correctly speaking, the prayers which preceded the clause of benediction:—"All Thy works and Thy pious people, the righteous who do Thy will, and Thy whole people, the house of Israel, ought to praise Thee, O Lord our God. With rejoicing ought they to acknowledge, bless, praise, celebrate, exalt, fear, sanctify, and glorify Thy name, O Thou our King; for it is right to praise Thee, and it is harmony to sing praises to Thy name: for from everlasting to everlasting Thou art God." Then the Benediction clause, which is attached to it, is, "Praised be Thou, O Lord, the King, glorified by laudations," was omitted, according to the best authorities and the approved custom on the Passover evening; because later, after the great Hallel, the blessing of the song followed, and it was unnecessary to multiply the benedictions, so similar in expression as the Hallel blessing and the blessing of the song.

In several editions of the Easter Haggada, the great Hallel follows immediately on the Hallel, while the Hallel blessing, "All Thy works," etc., comes in first after the blessing of the song. But then the clause of the blessing of the song is entirely omitted, as the Hallel blessing with its clauses are placed before and in place of the former. Other editions have the opposite, and entirely place the Hallel blessing after the Hallel, but close it with the usual benediction clause. The difference in relation to the addition or omission of this clause is noticed in the Babylonian Gemara with the direction to regulate this according to the custom of the place. The entire omission of the prayer, "All Thy works," etc., after the Hallel, and its insertion after the Blessing of the song, is in the *Tur Orach Chaijim* (§ 48i) attributed to the teaching of Saadias, which, however, has been controverted by his scholars.

After the Hallel, the so-called Great Hallel was sung. It has never been disputed that the 136th Psalm belonged to it. It is only doubtful whether, besides that, it contained other ingredients. In the Babylonian Gemara, three opinions are given. According to one, it consisted only of Psalm 136; according to another, Psalms 134, 135, and 136 (Psalms 120 to 136 can hardly be meant); according to a third, from 4th verse of Psalm 135 to end of Psalm 136. But in all cases the whole of Psalm 135 is meant, and only the more distinct intimation of it on account of the fourth verse given. Besides these, the Babylonian Gemara gives us a fourth very singular view as to the Great Hallel, according to which it should consist of Psalm 23. The Jerusalem Talmud, in its Mischna text, in a passage where the Babylonian Mischna text merely names the Great Hallel, makes the distinct assertion that it was Psalm 136. On this passage the Jerusalem Gemara has a long discussion about the Great Hallel, in which three opinions are brought forward. According to one it was Psalm 136; according to another, this and the preceding psalm; lastly, according to the singular opinion of Bar-kafra, it was the first three psalms of the Hallel, at the slaying of the Passover lamb in the temple. The third group was so little numerous that during the slaying of these lambs the whole Hallel could not be sung, but only that part of it. In the same passage there is a notice from what went before, that the Great Hallel was sung antiphonally, so that the cantor sang each time the first half of the verse, the assembly of those who remained the second half of the verse as a refrain. The responding of this same refrain seems, indeed, to have been already anticipated by the Prophet Jeremiah (xxxiii. 10). The present custom knows of no constituent part of the Great Hallel, except Psalm 136, although in an old Venetian edition of the Easter Haggada, before me now, this psalm follows Psalm 135.

The long hymnlike praise and thanksgiving, "The souls of all living praise Thy name," etc., was placed after the

Great Hallel, to which was added the blessing of the song alluded to in the beginning of a former paragraph. After two Easter songs, interpolated at a later period, and the wish, "Next year in Jerusalem" (which the old Venetian edition has at the end of the whole), the wine-blessing is spoken and the fourth cup drank. This has, however, as it is drank, after and beyond the supper-time, and the table-blessing does not apply to it, the following Benediction, in which God is thanked for the fruit of the vine and the bestowal of the Promised Land, with the prayer for their return thither. Later the ceremony was closed with a short hymn, which declared the termination of the prescribed solemnised Passover, and prayed for redemption. Still later there were added three popular hymns — two in Hebrew and one in Chaldee—which might also be sung in German.

The participation in four Passover cups was strictly prescribed, and it was not permitted to drink more except during the actual supper. But after the entire ceremony was over it was permitted to drink a fifth cup, but no man was considered bound to do so. If the fifth cup was to be drank, then it was necessary to omit the fourth before the great Hallel, and immediately to fill the fifth, recite the great Hallel and the blessing of the song over it, and to drink it with the same blessing which preceded and followed the fourth. This fifth cup is, however, nowhere mentioned in the Talmud; and the oldest authority known to me which says anything about this custom is the celebrated

Saadias, whom the *Tur Orach Chaijim* cites as discussing the fifth cup. The present custom ignores it altogether, although the old Venetian edition of the Easter Haggada, already noticed, mentions it.

§ 2. AGE OF THE JEWISH PASSOVER RITUAL.

Against the proposition that the ceremonial of the Passover evening reaches back to a very high antiquity, and substantially already existed at the time of the institution of the Lord's Supper, its complicated character ought not to be objected. For it is peculiar to all regulations which have developed themselves historically and organically, that they have the appearance of complication, while arbitrary elaboration at individual pleasure can very readily be simple. The best evidence for the true historical and traditional character of such Institutions lies, however, in this, that this appearance of complication on a close consideration always more and more disappears, and is replaced by a more simple and consistent fundamental character which has been in the course of centuries carefully worked out,—how simple is at bottom this Passover Ritual which appears so artificial and confused. The fundamental idea of the whole is the thankfulness to the God of Israel for the meat-offering and the symbolical deliverance from slavery which belongs to it. For the individual course of the ceremonial it is better to turn to the four Passover cups.

Over the first the consecration of the Festival is begun, and the day brought to one's conception as an uncommon day. Then the supper itself ought apparently to begin; but the question, if a child asks the reason of so many unwonted proceedings, obliges the father, over the second cup, to relate the works of God in carrying out the Exodus from Egypt, which brings him to the praise of God, which is done by the singing of psalms. As soon as the duty of a thankful remembrance of the wonderful deliverance has been fulfilled, the supper begins with a common eating of the food which symbolises the bitterness of the servitude and the grace of the deliverance. After the supper there is then the usual blessing of the table for those who have partaken, as well as for all earthly and higher benefits, which is pronounced over the third cup. But the heart is still so impressed with the wonderful greatness of the deliverance celebrated on this day, that its feelings can only be satisfied by the solemn chanting of the Hallel over the fourth cup, and the great Hallel which is connected with it, that majestic hymn which lauds the everlasting mercy of God as revealed in the creation, and in the wonderful conducting and delivering of His people, especially in the exodus from Egypt.

The possibility that the Passover Ritual already existed in the time of Christ and the apostles cannot be disputed, but its actual existence at that time ought yet to be proved by external evidence.

The strongest proof would self-evidently be derived from the indications in the New Testament of the particulars of the Passover celebration. We find, however, that such evidence is hardly to be found there. Even of the last Passover which our Lord celebrated with His disciples, the Apostles and Evangelists who describe it mention almost nothing of the ceremonial itself, for their whole interest was concentrated upon the Institution of the offering of the New Covenant at this festival. Besides this, communication regarding the Jewish Easter had little meaning for the Gentile Christians, while for the Jewish Christians they were superfluous. All that we can extract from the New Testament is confined to this, that they reclined at the table, which was moreover at that time the usual custom at their ordinary meals. Further, our Saviour by the expression, "Fruit of the vine," probably alludes to the blessing of the wine, and by the hymn which both St. Matthew and St. Mark mention at the close of the celebration, the Hallel may possibly be meant. On the other hand, a number of significant parallels break down under our hand. Thus we shall wonder that St. Luke does not speak of two different cups, but that on both occasions he means the one Eucharistic cup. In the same way the dipping of the sops in the dish for Judas does not belong to the Ritual, but took place at the earlier unceremonial part, or the supper.

On one side those who would hardly agree with the

evidence of a connection between the Jewish Passover Ritual and the primitive Christian Liturgy have, moreover, anxiously sought to show a similar connection for the most important and only substantial part of the Liturgy, viz. for the words of Institution, while exactly for these no connecting link with the Jewish Ritual is to be found. Such a connection has, however, been fancied, not purposely, but, as is so often the case, in such inquiries when a false view or misunderstanding has maintained a tenacious life during centuries, through a constant use of secondary authorities. In this manner has the opinion arisen that the words of Institution rested upon a usual formula at the distribution of the Paschal Lamb, "This is the body of the Passover." But this formula never existed, but rather the following Benediction preserved in the Tosiptha was said before the eating and giving of the flesh of the Easter Lamb, "Praised be Thou, O Lord our God, King of the world, that Thou hast sanctified us through Thy command, and hast commanded us to eat the Passover." For that other formula is rested on a later noticeable passage of the Mischna, where it is only said that in the time of the temple they had besides other food also "the body of the Passover," that is, brought in the unbroken, roasted, and served up Easter Lamb. This singular misunderstanding is found unaccountably even with the Talmudic scholar, Lightfoot, and has been ever since obstinately maintained.

As, then, the New Testament presents for our

inquiry little that we can take hold of, we must apply for information to the oldest post-biblical monuments of the Jewish literature. Josephus and Philo afford us likewise nothing tangible. We are therefore thrown almost entirely upon the declarations of the Mischna, and along with them the explanations laid down in the Gemara, as well as to bring together the scattered notices in the oldest Midrasch and other productions of the Talmudic period. If, then, the present Passover Ritual can be shown in its entirety in the Mischna, then its existence in the time of Christ and the Apostles is also proved; but there not only belonged to it several teachers whose discussions regarding the Passover solemnities are given in the Mischna during this and the preceding period, but it is also quite certain that the Halacha or the legal directions declared in an authoritative manner in the Mischna in substance had authority.

The relative section of the Mischna begins thus: At the Passover evening it was not allowed that anything should be eaten from the Mincha offering till dark, even a poor Israelite must not eat till he reclines at the Passover supper, and he must not be deprived of the four cups of wine, even though it had to be provided from the common chest. "After the first cup is mixed, the blessing must be spoken, according to the school of Schammai, first for the day, and then for the wine; but according to the school of Hillel, first for the wine, and then for the day." This last rule is adopted in the present practice, but the high antiquity of the Kiddusch spoken over the first cup is acknowledged, as already in the first century before Christ the different schools held disputations over it.

The Mischna proceeds thus: "There is brought before the president" (here several MSS. and the Jerusalem Talmud add "green herbs and lettice"). "He dips the lettice in before the bread has been eaten. There is brought before him unleavened bread, lettice, Charoseth, and two boiled dishes, although there is no command as to the Charoseth; Rabbi Elieser, son of Sadok, says, moreover, that it is a command. At the time of the temple there was brought also the body of the Passover." Here the bringing of the food and the apparent beginning of the supper is described as it is in the Easter Haggada, only instead of the green herbs, Charoseth, or lettice is mentioned, which the Mischna regards as one of the five kinds of bitter herbs, besides the *maror* or bitter herb in a narrower sense. It is beyond our object to attempt a solution of this apparent difference. Vinegar is not especially mentioned, but through the question of the child as to the twofold dipping, in which the Mischna text distinctly places against the simple dipping, implies it; it served at all events as sauce for the lettice, while the actual bitter herb, on account of its acidity, was dipped in the sweet Charoseth sauce.

About the second cup the Mischna says, "The second cup is then blessed," on which the son questions his father, and if the son has not yet understanding enough the father gives him guidance, "Why is this night different from all other nights," etc. The questions which follow agree with those already given, only the Mischna omits the question as to sitting and reclining; in the Jerusalem Talmud that also regarding the bitter herbs. After the questions it proceeds, "The father then instructs his son according to inquiry, he begins with the misery and closes with the praise, and he explains the passage, 'A wandering Aramæan was my father,' till he has finished the entire section." Rabban Gamabel was wont to say, "Whoever has not explained the following three things, viz. the Passover, the unleavened bread, and the bitter herbs, has not done his duty. The Passover, because God passed over the houses of our fathers in Egypt; the unleavened bread, because our fathers were delivered out of Egypt; the bitter herb, because the Egyptians made our fathers' lives in Egypt bitter." The Mischna then quotes the first half of the section given above, "In each generation," and the entire following, "Therefore are we guilty," down to the "and let us say Hallelujah before Him." Then it remarks with regard to the first part of the Hallel and the closing Benediction to the Haggada, "The school of Schammai sings the Hallel to the end of Psalm cxiii., the school of Hillel to the end of Psalm cxiv." The Benediction which follows has one of the clauses relative to the deliverance. Rabbi Tarson says indeed, only, "That Thou hast delivered us and our fathers out of Egypt" (the Jerusalem Talmud adds "and hast allowed us to survive this night "), and added no clause of blessing to it. But Rabbi Akiba says further, "So may our God and the God of our fathers allow us to survive in peace to other times and festivals which we expect, joyful over the rebuilding of Thy city and rejoicing over Thy service, and may we there eat of the sacrifices and the Passover offering?" and so on to the clause of blessing, "Praised be Thou, O Lord, that Thou hast delivered Israel."

The Mischna mentions nothing of the Chaldaic beginning, which looked at from the last words appears to be old. The question which follows is at all events extremely old, as the notice of the Easter Lamb proves. So far as regards the actual Haggada, it cannot to a word be placed in the time of the Mischna as it is at present, for the father should instruct the son according to his judgment and understanding. Still not only the two last sections of the Hallel existed already at that time in their present form, but all that went before had in the Mischna its strictly regulated succession and norm, although the present expressions of the Easter Haggada suit sometimes the relative passages of the Mischna. There are especially many passages of our Haggada taken from the oldest Midrasch, reaching back to the third century after Christ, viz. the "Sipri," a commentary upon Numbers and Deuteronomy and the "Mechiltha," a fragmentary commentary upon Exodus. What concerns the one, the beginning of the Haggada resting upon Deut. vi. 21, is proved by the Babylonian

Gemara. The assertion which Rabbi Eleazar makes as to the duty of relating the exodus in the night from Egypt is taken from the Mischna. The remarks as to the four different questioners pointed out in the Thora spring first from the Mechiltha, which on its part has taken them from the Jerusalem Gemara. Meanwhile at the time the Babylonian Gemara was compiled all this must already have been contained in the Haggada, for the Gemara teachers' dispute, whether the "misery" of which, according to the direction of the Mischna, the relater should first speak refers to the mention of the servitude in Egypt in the beginning of the Haggada or to the mention of the heathenism of the forefathers of Abraham which now follows it. This dispute would have been an irrelevant one had there not been passages of another kind between the two regarding the misery. The explanation of the twenty-sixth chapter of Deuteronomy 5–9 was already prescribed in the Mischna, still they seem earlier with more freedom, not to have been given according to a strictly fixed formulary; for many of the explanations in the present Haggada are manifestly again borrowed from the Sifri, Mechiltha, and similar books. The explanations of this section are succeeded by a long analysis full of trifling, refining, acuteness of the plagues of the Egyptians, and the relative benefits to the Israelites, which are in part found in the Mechiltha, the Midrasch to the Psalms, and other works, and probably interpolated at a late period, as Maimonides does not mention them. The explanations regarding the Paschal lamb, the unleavened bread, and the bitter herbs are already prescribed in the Mischna, while, on the other hand, the words in the present Haggada introductory to those explanations are taken from the relative passages in the Mischna. The two last sections, as already remarked, are given *verbatim*. The contents and arrangements of the Easter Haggada, as indicated by the Mischna, agree entirely with our present text. On the other hand, there are many interpolations not to be mistaken, and also in the greater part of the others the exact expression has been fixed at a late period.

There is again a difference of opinion mentioned between Hillel and Schammai as to the first part of the Hallel, in relation to which the practice as usual follows the former. The Benediction for the deliverance of Israel which follows this part of the Hallel and closed the entire Haggada was originally a "short" one, that is, had not a twofold "Praised be Thou," one at the beginning, the other at the close; Rabbi Akiba, towards the beginning of the second century after Christ, first enlarged it by a prayer for the rebuilding of Jerusalem and the restoration of the temple worship, and as the blessing became thus more complete added at the end a benediction clause. The first part of the blessing which does not refer to the rebuilding of Jerusalem appears to be very old.

The conclusion of the Passover Ritual is thus given in the Mischna, "The third cup is then mixed, the blessing of the table is spoken over it; over the fourth the Hallel is completed, and the blessing of the song said over it. Any one who would drink between the cups may do so, but between the third and the fourth cup no one must drink. No Asikoman is taken after the Passover."

Our sources do not very distinctly specify the ceremonies to be observed at the supper. They are, however, self-evident, and we find them outside of the Passover festival. The blessing of the bread, for instance, over two cakes held on high takes place at each festival; the peculiarity of the Passover blessing consists in this, that one of the cakes is broken. On the other hand, the custom is mentioned that a portion of the Paschal lamb is eaten as the last morsel, in its place later the Asikoman came in, the preserved half of an unleavened cake. The blessing of the table over the third cup is also mentioned. There is in the Gemara of the treatise Berachoth a full discussion as to its single constituent parts, where not only the introductory responses mentioned in the Mischna appear, but also even the Benediction of the feeder of all is brought to act upon Moses, that on the land upon Joshua, that upon Israel, Jerusalem and the Temple upon David and Solomon, while the prayer which follows the benediction for the building of Jerusalem, which praises God as the good and giver of good according to the same source, must have been added in the period after Christ. On the other hand, it looks at first sight as if the Hallel only and not also the great Hallel was sung over the fourth cup, while the Gemara fully deals with both. When, however, the words of the Mischna are more closely weighed, viz. the expression "Blessing of the song," one sees that the great Hallel is clearly indicated in it. The Hallel is followed by, not the blessing of the song, but another blessing peculiar to the Hallel, which is placed after it on the Passover evening, but in order not to multiply too much the benedictions without the clause of benediction. Now as the Mischna makes the Hallel to be followed, not by the blessing of the Hallel, but by the blessing of the song, which is prayed after the singing of other psalms, and has its name from the following words in its clause, "That Thou willingly accepted the songs of the Church," it follows of necessity that there was a psalm chanted after the Hallel and before the blessing of the song, and this can only be in the great Hallel distinctly prescribed by the Gemara at this place.

The Gemara also mentions the prayer after the Hallel, and remarks that its Benediction clause was spoken by some, omitted by others; further, the long introduction beginning with "the souls of all living," which preceded, on the Passover evening as well as at the Sabbath morning prayer, the blessing of the song. Some passages in this introduction may be later interpolations. On the other hand, we contest most decidedly the removal of the blessing of the song itself to the Saboraic period, as long as Zunz brings forward no ground for this opinion.[39] The prayer "The soul of all living" is merely an introduction to the blessing of the song, and is already mentioned in the Talmud. How then can the blessing of the song itself be a product of the Saboraic time.

The Mischna mentions supplementally that over the Passover Lamb and the Chagiga a blessing was also spoken. No words were added in the Tosiphtha.

We have thus persuaded ourselves that the sources which most truly represent the ritualistic traditions and observances among the Jews in the time of Christ and the apostles in relation to the celebration of the Passover supper, in almost every particular agree with the present Easter Haggada, and have, moreover, the right to use this, but after deducting some later interpolated constituents and the alterations rendered necessary from the cessation of the temple service, for our comparison with the primitive Christian Liturgy.

§ 3. THE SABBATH-MORNING PRAYER.

As in the closing part of our treatise we have to compare the primitive Christian pre-communion with the Jewish Schacharith, or morning prayer for the Sabbath, we must here give a complete representation of it, we might, indeed, confine ourselves to the last part of it from the lessons out of the Mosaic law to the end, as it is at that point that the parallel with the Christian

---

[39] Zunz, *Literatur geschichte der Synagogue*, sec. 12.

Eucharistic service begins. Still we ought not to leave the previous part entirely unconsidered, as it is mainly from it that we must take the evidence for the high antiquity of this prayer.

It is known that the Mosaic law, with the exception of the priestly blessing over the people, prescribes no fixed liturgical formulary, but only holy actions, the bringing of bloody and unbloody offerings and incense for the temple service. Still, according to the Talmud, there were connected with the morning and evening sacrifice fixed prayers and the chanting of one of the seven psalms appropriated to each day of the week. That such chanting of psalms frequently resounded in the temple, and that the people took part in the same, with Amen and other responses, appears from the sacred authors both before and after the time of Christ.

At all events from the Babylonian exile there were fixed times of prayer and congregations for prayer outside of the temple, though in connection with the temple worship; so that the two most important times of prayer, the Schacharith and the Mincha, correspond with the two daily sacrifices—the morning sacrifice, and the Mincha as afternoon sacrifice. On Sabbaths and festivals there were special festival sacrifices added to the daily sacrifices. They were on those days represented by the temple prayers, which were added to the morning prayer. Besides this the Arbith or evening prayer was also observed.

The Schacharith of the Sabbath begins as always

with the morning Benedictions, which consist of praise, thanks, and prayer, and with which are connected some biblical and Talmudic lessons as to the daily sacrifice; upon this follows the psalmody, which consists of the Davidic song, pointed out in 1 Paralip. xvi. 18-36, taken from a foregoing benediction, a psalm cento, and the 100th Psalm; after a prayer placed between them the six last psalms are recited, a short praising of God is added, and then after an introduction recited standing, the hymn of Moses (Ex. xv.), and the psalmody closes with the blessing of the song. On Sabbaths and festivals instead of the 100th Psalm, Psalms xix., xxxiv., xc., cxxxv., cxxxvi., xxxiii., xcii., and xciii. are sung and precede the blessing of the song, which we already know from the Passover ritual, the hearty praising, "The souls of all living." After this the so-called half or small Kaddisch is prayed, which, on a call from the cantor, to the praise of God, is spoken by one of the congregation, with the praise beginning "Praised and glorified is," and consists of the words added by the cantor and congregation together, "Praised be the blessed Lord for ever and ever." Then follows the recitation of the Schma, a combination of the striking Thora words, Deut. vi. 4-9, xi. 13-22; and Numb. xv. 37-41. Before it there is a long and splendid Benediction of God as creator of light, and a short one for the choosing of the people of Israel; after this Schma follows a Benediction of God as the deliverer of Israel. In the Middle Ages there were many festival hymns or puttim composed, which were thrust in at certain passages of the benedictions, which preceded and followed the Schma as well as the Schmone Esre.

Upon this were said, "Lord, open my lips and my mouth shall show forth Thy praise," and the Schmone Esre, or eighteen Benedictions, which is also termed "the prayer" in a narrower sense, is begun. At present there are nineteen, because in the first century after Christ a prayer for the destruction of heretics and apostates was interpolated after the eleventh benediction.

These prayers contain the acknowledgment of God's protection of Israel, the resurrection of the dead, the holiness of God, thanks for the gift of reason, repentance, and the forgiveness of sins, the prayer for deliverance, health, and fruitful harvests; also a series of prayers for the Messianic salvation; lastly, a thanksgiving for the regular care of God for His people, and the prayer for peace. Before the last prayer of the Schmone Esre, relating to peace, if a descendent of Aaron is present, the priestly blessing prescribed in Num. vi. 24 is given. When saying the blessing the priest holds up his hands over the congregation, who stand before him, with eyes directed to the floor. In the Portuguese rite the priestly blessing is given every Sabbath; in the German, only on certain festival days. If no priest is present, the blessing will not be given, but only referred to. On Sabbaths and festival days only the first three and last three prayers of Schmone Esre are prayed, as a Benediction appropriate to the Sabbath or the festival is interpolated. On Sabbaths, however, as well as on week-days, the Keduscha is inserted at the third Benediction of the Schmone Esre, which has a striking resemblance to the Preface and Sanctus. The cantor says, for instance, at the Sabbath-morning prayer, "Let us hallow Thy name on earth, as it is hallowed in heaven; as is written in the prophets, The one called to the other, and said,"—here the people respond, "Holy, holy, holy is the Lord of Sabaoth; the whole earth is full of Thy glory." The cantor then says, "Thus raise thy voices with great, glorious, and hearty chants, they raise them over against the Seraphim, and sing in alternative chorus, Praised be He"—on which the congregation answer, "Praised be the glory of the Lord from out of its place." The conclusion is, "In thy holy Scriptures it is written;" with the response, "May the Lord govern for ever, thy God, O Zion, from generation to generation. Hallelujah."

What follows of the morning prayer will be presented in a clear light if regarded with reference to the Sabbath-morning service only; for on week-days the varying lessons from the Mosaic law and the prophets do not take place (only on Mondays and Thursdays the beginning of Thora section read on Sabbath is anticipated), and thus the last part of the Sabbath-morning prayer assumes a different aspect from that on the week-days.

On Sabbath, after the shortened Schmone Esre is completed, the roll of the Thora is taken out of the ark and brought to the reading-desk, accompanied by several prayers and Responsory praise. After the reading, there follows a praise of the Book of the Law, beginning with the words, "This is the law laid before the Israelites by Moses." The reading of the Parascha, or the varying chapters out of the books of Moses read on the Sabbath, was wont to be done by several members selected from the congregation, who were called one after another to the reading-desk, and each time pronounced a Benediction before and after it. After the Parascha was finished, and the half Kaddisch prayed, the Haftara was read; a similar varying portion of the prophetical writings to which Jews, as is known, reckoned also the Books of Joshua, the Judges, Samuel, and Kings. The Haftara was introduced by two Benedictions, the second of which was also a closing Benediction for the Mosaic lesson. Several others followed the Haftara, which partly praised God for the truth and certainty of His word, and partly prayed Him to fulfil the promises of the prophets, to have mercy on Zion, and to restore the government of the house of David. After the Haftara an explanatory or hortatory discourse was held.

Upon this followed reading the Intercessions. First, the following prayer in the Chaldean language was said: "It is on behalf of salvation from heaven, grace, favour, and mercy, long life and rich support of life, heavenly help, health of body and light from above, healthy and strong successors, which shall not cease and neglect the study of the law, our Lord and Rabbi, the Holy College in the land of Israel and in Babylon, the professors, princes of the exile, academy rectors, and judges at the door—all these disciples and all disciples of their disciples, and all who study the law. The King of the world bless them, lengthen their lives, multiply their days, and give to their years continuance, and may they be freed and saved from all oppression and all hostile cunning. Our Lord in heaven preserve them each time and hour. Let us say, Amen." A second Chaldaic prayer agrees *verbatim* with the foregoing, except that it does not pray for the Scribes and Presidents, but for "this holy congregation, large and small, children and women."

The next Intercession is again compiled in Hebrew, and runs thus: "He who has blessed our fathers Abraham, Isaac, and Jacob, may He bless this holy congregation, with all other holy congregations, them and their wives, and sons and daughters, and all which belongs to Him; even so those who have assembly houses for prayer, and those who frequent them in order to pray; further, those who present lamps for lighting them and wine for the Kiddusch and the Habdala (these are, as already remarked, the usual blessings spoken at the beginning and end of the Sabbath), and bread for travellers, and alms for the poor, and all who exert themselves with fidelity for the interests of the congregation. The Holy One, the Blessed One repay them the reward, and remove from them all sickness, and heal their bodies, and forgive them their sins, and send blessing and increase on all work of their hands, and on all Israel, their brethren; and let us say, Amen."

At this point the following prayer is added, if a woman who is lying-in comes for the first time again to the Synagogue, or a sick person is prayed for. The first proceeds thus: "Thou who hast blessed our father Abraham, Isaac, and Jacob, bless this mother (*N. N.*), along with her new-born son, with good produce, for the sake of the alms with which her husband has commended for both; as a reward, therefore, may the son grow up to the law, and to marriage, and to good works." The prayer for the sick begins in the same manner: "Thou who hast blessed our fathers Abraham, Isaac, and Jacob, Moses and Aaron, David and Solomon, do Thou heal the sick (*N. N.*) for the sake of the gift with which (*N. N.*) has commended for him. For a reward for that, may the Holy One, the Praised One, have mercy upon him, make him well, strengthen, alter, and renovate him, and may He send him perfect recovery from heaven in all his limbs and nerves, along with the other sick in Israel, healing of the soul and body now and soon; and let us say, Amen." Moreover, these Intercessions for lying-in women and the sick, commonly inserted in that said for each reader of the Thora, likewise beginning with the words, "Thou who has blessed," while the relative, husband, or relation is called for the Thora.

On the Sabbath after the new moon, which follows the festivals of Easter and of Tabernacles, a quite similar

Intercession is said for those who have undertaken to fast on Monday and Thursday. In some congregations this Intercession for those who fast is inserted in the last portion of the general intercession for the benevolent and giver of alms.

After this, the prayer for the king is said. And with this is connected, in many congregations on each Sabbath, in others only on the day of atonement, and in some others on the highest festivals, the prayer for the dead. The prayer for deceased relatives is thus expresssed: "May God remember the souls of my father and mother, my grandfather and grandmother, my brothers and sisters, my relatives on the father's and mother's side who have passed into their eternity. For the sake of the alms which I commend for them, may their souls be included in the bundle of life with the souls of Abraham, Isaac, and Jacob, Sara, Rebecca, Rachel, Leah, and the other righteous men and women in the Garden of Eden; and let us say, Amen." With the same words are those remembered who have been put to death for their faith. In honour of these another prayer, beginning with the words, "The Father of Mercies," is added.

On the Sabbath before the new moon, after the other Intercessions, a prayer is added, in which God is prayed "to renew this month over us for good and for blessing, and to give us abundant life, a life of peace, a life of good, a life of blessing, a life of nourishment, a life of riches and honour, a life in which the desire of our hearts to good will be fulfilled. Amen." This prayer, according to the treatise Berachoth (fol. 16b), proceeds from the well-known Rab, the founder of the Jewish law school at Babylon towards the beginning of the third century.

After the conclusion of the Intercessions, Ps. cxlv. is sung. Then the cantor takes the Book of the Law back to the ark, and says, "Praised be the name of the Lord, for His name alone is high;" upon which the congregation answer, "His glory is spread over heaven and earth, and He raises the horn of His people; to Him be praise from His pious ones, from Israel, the people that stand near Him. Hallelujah." Then Ps. xxix. is sung (on week-days, in which there is reading out of the Law, it is Ps. xxiv.), and the Schacharith is closed with a short prayer which accompanies the laying of the Book of the Law in the ark.

The Musaph prayer follows immediately on the Schacharith. It consists, in the same manner as in the morning prayer, of a shortened Schmone Esre. Between the first three and the last three Benedictions there is one appropriate to the Sabbath introduced, and in this the extraordinary sacrifice prescribed for the Sabbath is mentioned. The Keduscha begins in Musaph with the words, "With reverend fear we would praise Thy holiness as with the mysterious utterance of the holy seraphim who glorify Thy name in holiness," etc.; after a lesson from the Talmud as to the bringing of the incense in the temple there follows at the end of all the offices the prayer ascribed to Rab, "The one duty to praise," etc., which expresses the acknowledgment of the unity of God and the hope of the destruction of idolatry, along with a complete Kaddisch which contains responses in the Chaldee language between the cantor and the congregation, and the first half of which forms the before-mentioned small Kaddisch. The first responses of the Kaddisch have a great resemblance to the prayers at the beginning of the Lord's Prayer; those that follow pray for the prayers of the people being heard, and for peace for Israel, with the chanting of Ps. xcii., which at the time of the temple was the psalm of the day for the Sabbath, and with the Kaddisch prayed by one of the orphans left behind for rest to the souls of their parents the united Schacharith and Musaph is closed on Sabbath.

That the canonical times of the day of the Jews, like the Passover ritual, existed in the time of Christ and of the apostles in their present form (the three hours of prayer were already noticed in the Book of Daniel, vi. 11, 12), appears evidently from the Mischna of the Talmud treatise on the benedictions. In it there is not only mentioned the four times of prayer, Schacharith, Musaph, Mincha, and Arhith,[40] but also the placing together of the Schma and the Schmone Esre is spoken of in a manner that its full agreement with the present text cannot be disputed. So far as regards the Schma, the Mischna mentions the three Mosaic

---

[40] Tr. Berachoth fol. 26a.

passages from which it is put together, as well as the opening words of the prayers attached to it; further, it says that two benedictions preceded the Schma in Schacharith and in Arhith; there followed it, however, in Schacharith only that one the beginning of which is given last in Arhith too, a long and a short one. This description shows so clearly the existence of the present Schma prayer at the time of the Mischna instructor, that we do not miss a distinct representation of the rest, as we find it in the Gemara. Moreover, Haneberg[41] has shown that the first prayer before the Schma in Schacharith, which praises God as the Creator of light, on account of its thorough polemic bearing upon the Persian Dualism and the representation of the Amschaspands, reaches back to a still greater antiquity, and must belong to the first century after the return from the Babylonian captivity. That the Schmone Esre, which according to the treatise Megilla was brought in through the great synagogue already in the time of the Mischna, resembled the present, is implied by its name, but still more decidedly from the following passage: "It mentions the rain shower, although resurrection of the dead (in the second prayer of the Schmone Esre) and rain is prayed for in the blessing of the year (in the ninth prayer, which prays for a fruitful harvest). It notices the Haddala in those favoured with judgment (at the end of a Sabbath or festival the Haddala blessing, which relates to the distinction between holy and

---

[41] *Religiose Alterthumer der Bibel*, § 359.

common days, is inserted before the close of the fourth benediction: "Praised be Thou, Lord, that Thou favourest with judgment," etc.).[42] The second last benediction and the thanksgiving prayer belonging to it, "We acknowledge before Thee," are numbered in the same passage. While Gamaliel teaches in the Mischna that one must pray the eighteen Schmone Esre every day, Akiba is contented with an extract from it. The nature of this extract is more closely given in the Gemara, and it is mentioned that on Sabbaths and festivals the first three and last three benedictions are retained, and between them a seventh, appropriate to the day, inserted. This arrangement is already set forth in the Mischna of the treatise Rosch haschana (fol. 32a). Here the Schmone Esre on new year's day is thus described; after the first three prayers, which take their name from their leading word, comes the insertion peculiar to the day; then the last three prayers, termed service, confession, and priestly blessing. The Gemara informs us further that the additional prayer after the eleventh benediction against the flight to Jamnia was added at Gamaliel's instance, and indicates the verse of the psalm which introduces the Schmone Esre.[43] Lastly, the Talmud mentions the bestowing of the Aaronite blessing before the last prayer of the Schmone Esre.[44]

The particulars of the morning prayer, which we have

---

[42] Tr. Berachoth, fol. 28*b*, 33*a*.
[43] *Ibid.* fol. 4*b*, 9*b*.
[44] Tr. Sota fol. 39*a* *b*; Tr. Megilla, fol. 18*a*.

hitherto described, do not come, with the exception of the Schmone Esre of the Musaph, into the sphere which in our opinion shows accordance with the antecommunion, but still as old proved constituent parts of the morning prayer they afford us a not unimportant evidence for the rest. For the Mosaic and prophetical lessons indeed, with which the most important part of the Schacharith for us begins, we do not require to appeal to this evidence. We can here turn our eyes even from the Mischna, because the New Testament itself gives us the strongest proof of the reading of Paraschin and Haftara. St. James points out (Acts xv. 21) that the books of Moses of old time had been read in every Synagogue on the Sabbath day. Josephus also informs us that the Jews assembled in each week to hear the reading of the law.[45] The reading of the Haftara appears also from the proceedings of our Lord in the synagogue at Capernaum, related by St. Luke (iv. 16). A passage in the Acts of the Apostles (xiii. 14) instructs us also as to the order in which the lessons were read. First the Parascha out of the Book of the Law was read, after this the prophetical Haftara, to which was wont to be attached the sermon.

It is true that we can produce fewer old testimonies for the intercession prayers which follow, and which are of the utmost importance for our object. Much, in fact, to be found in them can only belong to it after the destruction of the temple. We are, however, persuaded

[45] *Contra Apionem*, 217.

that those passages which in the present text betray later views and arrangements, still at an earlier period expressed substantially the same contents only in a different manner. So is it certain that in the time of the second temple instead of or along with the intercession for the Rabbis and scribes, another must have been in use for the priesthood. At all events we have the right to hold the intercessions as old in their substantial contents and series, and to compare them with Christian intercessions with which they are in accord, as long as their later compilation cannot be proved on positive grounds. The circumstance that in the passage of the Acts of the Apostles already referred to it is so distinctly indicated that after the conclusion of the lessons out of the law and the prophets strangers present are called upon to preach a sermon, seems, moreover, to speak for this, that after these lessons a substantial part of the Sabbath-morning service was still to follow; for otherwise the time of the sermon would have been more simply indicated (Acts xiii. 43), perhaps by before the congregation was dismissed. The Schulchan Aruch (Orach Chaijim, 284. 7), compiled in the sixteenth century, first mentions distinctly our intercessions, where he refers to Mordechai Bar Rabbi Hillel, living in the thirteenth century, "After the reading of the Thora it was usual to remember the dead, and bless those who had taken upon themselves the functions of the congregation. Each place did this according to their custom. The prayer 'From heaven is in part' was wont to be said, by which the prohibition of petitioning intercession on the Sabbath was not disregarded. The prayer 'Father of Mercies' was also said in honour of the martyrs," etc.

That these Intercessions, notwithstanding the very slender evidence, must be of great antiquity, appears from this, that in the ritual used for the consecration of the princes of the exile, which is known partly through a report of the Babylonian Nathan (tenth century) preserved in the Book Juchasin, partly from a judgment of the first Gaonen time, made use of by the editor of the Schebit Jehuda, Grätz[46] has shown that this last source must have been compiled while rectors of the academy were dependent on the princes of the exile, some time before 825; for the judgment reports that the rectors had read out of the Thora to the prince of the exile, while Nathan asserts that they had not read on this occasion in order not to appear as subjects of the princes of the exile. The judgment contained in the forty-second chapter of the Schebit Jehuda relates that the prince of the exile on the first Sabbath after his consecration, after the conclusion of the lessons from the Scriptures, must preach a sermon and then have a collection for the academy. The prince of the exile then prayed for the rectors of the academy, further for doers of good deeds and givers of alms, also for those who took care of the affairs of the congregation, then for particular lands, their preservation from

[46] *Geschichte der Juden*, v. § 458.

war, contagious diseases, and other plagues, and for the coming of the Messianic salvation. After that they betook themselves to a festival meal in the house of the prince of the exile. From this description it follows that both the Chaldaic and the first Hebrew intercessions had already in the eighth century their present position and form, as the sermon preceded them.

This circumstance brings us to the same result, that the order of prayer established in the ninth century by the Gaon Amram contains almost *verbatim* these intercessions, especially the Chaldaic "From heaven in part," as well as that the Karaites who separated from Rabbinism in the eighth century, who rejected the Talmudic Rabbinic tradition, but not the general religious practice, have likewise intercessions at the end of the Sabbath-morning prayer, and in substance the same which we now find with the Rabbinists.[47]

There are celebrated in them the remembrance of the deceased founders and teachers of this character; further come prayers for the whole community, for those who conduct the prayers and the lessons, for the Lord of the land, the givers of alms, the officers of the community, the learned, the sick, the lying-in women, and other accidental petitions.

For the remembrance of souls we have a particular evidence in the Midrasch Tanchuma on the Pentateuch (probably composed in the ninth century), wherein it is said, "It is necessary to pray on the Sabbath for the

---

[47] Comp. Jost, *Geschichte der Judenthums*, ii. § 317.

dead, in order that it may not be necessary for them again to return to hell." This passage confirms also the statement of the Schulchan Aruch and other older authorities, that prayers for the dead were said every Sabbath; the narrower use which is now frequently made of them must be a novelty.

We may thus with certainty carry our Intercessions as far back as the eighth century. It is even probable that some of them in their present form cannot be much older. At all events, the Chaldaic prayer presupposes the existence of the dignity of Exilarch and the academy constitution which perfected itself in Babylon in the third century. That the contents of all those prayers must substantially be of primitive antiquity appears from their perfect agreement with the Christian Liturgy, and cannot through any argument *e silentio* lose their force.

III.

COMPARISON OF THE APOSTOLIC LITURGY WITH THE ACCORDANT JEWISH RITUAL.

§ 1. THE INSTITUTION OF THE HOLY EUCHARIST IN ITS CONNECTION WITH THE PASSOVER SUPPER.

As we are now approaching more nearly the ultimate object of our inquiry, to which all that went before was merely a circumstantial, but for the understanding of what follows, an indispensably necessary introduction, it hardly requires the distinct remark that it in no way deals with the present form of the holy Eucharist as in any respect to be derived from Jewish usages or formularies. This present form, the mysterious words of institution of our Lord, through which bread and wine become His body and blood, is, much more something quite new, a miracle of the love of God revealed in Christ, for which all connecting links in the Old Covenant are wanting. We will not renew the attempt undertaken from the extra-ecclesiastical side, and already rejected in the preceding part, to explain the words of institution from the Passover ritual, but merely show that the ceremonies, prayers, and thanksgivings, which stand in closer relation to the oblation perfected by the consecration, connect themselves in their arrangements in the order of the parts, and still more in their expressions with the Passover feast, during which our Saviour instituted the sacrifice of the New Covenant. This thought lies, from what goes before, so close to us that one must really wonder at the slight attention which has been bestowed upon it by the liturgists. For as it is certain that the Saviour instituted the holy Eucharist during the celebration of the Passover, that is, the present constituent parts of the Eucharist, the consecration and communion, by the first offering, of which necessarily other parts of the Passover ritual must have partly preceded it partly followed; as, further, the apostles as they fixed the order of the Liturgy for the use of the Church certainly as much as possible adhered to the form used by their Divine Master in the first institution of it, not only in relation to the words of institution, but also in relation to the whole celebration,—so might we expect that the apostolic Liturgy would, independently of the actual words of consecration, correspond in the greater part with the Passover ritual.

There arises here, indeed, the question whether the Divine Redeemer really instituted the holy Eucharist after the Passover supper on the 14th Nisan, or whether this assumption, upon which the whole hypothesis we maintain as to the origin of the primitive Christian Liturgy rests, is not a mistaken one. The reader, however, need not be afraid that a reiterated revision of the disputed question, so many times discussed, as to the day of the crucifixion, will be here attempted. For so decidedly are we of opinion that the Saviour, according to the unmistakable testimony of the first three evangelists, celebrated the Passover with His disciples on the evening of the 14th Nisan, and at this time instituted the holy Eucharist; consequently the apparently contradictory statement of St. John has to be brought into accord with it, and not the reverse; still there enters among the numerous solutions only one that would come into collision with our proposition of a connection between the Jewish Easter celebration and the primitive Christian Liturgy, viz. that according to which Christ did not anticipate the Passover on the 13th Nisan, but held an ordinary supper for the institution of the Eucharist. In the most forced manner the defenders of this view refer the words of Christ as to His longing desire to partake of the Passover with His disciples, not to the true Easter lamb, but only to the holy Eucharist itself. But against this the narrative of the first three evangelists speaks too plainly, according to which the disciples on the day when the Passover must be slain asked Jesus in what place they should prepare the Passover supper, on which they made the necessary preparations, and then as the hour came reclined at table with their Divine Master. All these particulars declare so incontrovertibly against the perversion of this view, which holds that the Last Supper of Jesus was an ordinary meal, that it is now universally recognised as untenable, and in this century, so far as we know, has not found a single defender. We can therefore give this hypothesis over to a merited oblivion; the others, however, as they in no way conflict with our hypothesis, may remain at rest. To those, however, who may wish to instruct themselves thoroughly on this question, we can recommend as the newest and best defence of the right view, Lange's *Letze Lebenstage Jesu*, and the work of Kirchner, *Die Judische Paschafeier und Jesu Letzes Mahl*.[48]

As the entire connection of the Jewish Easter ritual with the primitive Christian Liturgy depends upon the institution of the holy Eucharist taking place at the Passover evening, so an exhaustive inquiry into this connection must begin by ascertaining the precise position which the consecration occupied in the last Passover supper of Jesus. We have one certain indication of this in the distinct statement of the Apostle Paul and of St. Luke, that the consecration of the cup took place after the supper, so that the first and second cups, as well as the unritual drinking during the supper, are at all events excluded. Many have held that the

[48] [The apparent contradiction between the narrative of St. John and that of the Synoptists arises from an imperfect acquaintance with Jewish antiquities, and of the meaning of the terms employed by the Jews. This was clearly pointed out by Lightfoot in his Talmudic Commentary. As the Passover supper was eaten after six o'clock, a ceremonial taint, which lasted only till the end of the day, could not have prevented the Jews eating, and St. John applies the term of Passover to the Chagiga eaten next forenoon.—Tr.]

third cup was the Eucharistic one, founding upon the fact that St. Paul gives the same name to the Eucharistic cup as the Rabbis to the third Passover cup, viz. "The cup of blessing;" but this resemblance is only verbal, while the meaning in the cases is totally different. The Rabbis received the four cups according to what was recited before they were drank; the first they called the cup of the Kiddusch or consecration of the feast; the second, the cup of the Haggada; the fourth, the cup of the Hallel; and in like manner the third, the cup of the blessing of the table, or shortly, the cup of blessing, only because the usual prayer after meals preceded it. St. Paul, however, names the Eucharistic cup the cup of blessing, because the thanksgiving for creation and redemption, closing with the consecration, was said over it. It is also improbable that Christ should have brought the institution of this most holy Sacrament into connection with the daily thanksgiving prayer for earthly nourishment which follows every meal, as it was open to Him to use the fourth cup for this purpose, over which the solemn Hallel used on festival days only, with its striking contents, was sung. Lastly, the time indicated by the expression "after the supper," makes it almost impossible that it could have been the third cup, as this, being the cup of the blessing of the table, formed the conclusion of the supper, but still belonged to it. This conclusion is manifest from the ritual; for as little over the third cup as over the first and the second was a following blessing of the wine said, but the blessing of the table was sufficient for them, while each independent cup, and therefore also the fourth, which came after supper, and was separated from it, was followed by another blessing in addition to the blessing which preceded it.

There remains therefore only the fourth cup, or, if one will, the fifth voluntary cup, as possible for the Eucharistic cup. The comparison of the Passover ritual with the Liturgy later on will show that the first view is by far the most probable, to which may be added that the fifth cup is first mentioned in the tenth century, and appears to be a custom which arose long after the time of Christ. Langen's objection, that Christ, who perfectly observed the law, was not likely to mix up the Passover rite with the Eucharistic, is relieved by this, that the four cups were prescribed, not by the divine law, but only by the authority of the scribes; and further, that the Passover rite was not given up, but rather fulfilled in that higher rite which came to it, and that even, according to Langen's view, towards the end of the celebration a concurrent proceeding of the Easter and the eucharistic ritual was to be accepted.

As to the closer question at what particular part of the Hallel, or of that part still to be recited over the fourth cup, the words of consecration were inserted, St. Luke gives us the clearest explanation. The striking words of the evangelist have been generally misunderstood, because it was believed that he here speaks of two different cups. This is, however, not to be thought of, for the mention of a ritual cup preceding the Eucharistic cup as something standing by itself and of no importance for the evangelic history could have no object; fully, however, because the bringing forward of one of these three cups and making no mention of the other two is utterly incomprehensible, and without motive. Besides this, St. Luke makes the divine Redeemer at first taking the cup say the words, "Take this, and divide it among yourselves; for I say unto you, I will not drink of the fruit of the vine until the kingdom of God shall come," which plainly agrees closely with the words mentioned by the other evangelists immediately before the form of consecration, "Take this, and drink ye all of it;" and then the same words follow about not drinking from the fruit of the vine. Lastly, the command, according to which the same cup should be used by all, shows that it then held consecrated wine. For at the Passover supper each person drank out of his own cup, and the opinion that occasionally one cup was handed around is an arbitrary assumption of modern learned men derived from the New Testament, which has no foundation in any Jewish source. Much more, as we shall afterwards see, was the command of Jesus, that all should drink out of the same cup, a quite uncommon one, and warranted by the circumstance that it was only over this cup that the consecration had been completed. If, therefore, we learn in relation to a single cup mentioned at Jesus's last Passover supper, that it was handed round, we have to hold it without further discussion for the Eucharistic cup.

That St. Luke speaks only of one, and that the Eucharistic cup, is recognised by Langen; but he is of the mistaken opinion that the evangelist presents the circumstance with a certain obscurity and confusion, while we, on the other hand, obtain only from him a clear insight into the place of the words of institution within the Passover ritual. We learn, namely, from his representation, that Jesus before the consecration of the bread took the fourth cup to be later consecrated, and made to His disciples two relative communications in regard to it, in order not to interrupt the consecration and communion which followed by any external rules for their conduct or answers to questions. At first He directs them to drink out of the same cup, which will be afterwards consecrated, so that they might divide the contents among themselves in contrast to the usual custom by which each used his own cup. Besides this, He informed them of His intention, not Himself to drink along with them out of this cup equally, in order to prevent, if possible, reaching the cup here and there during communion.

As we have recognised the fourth cup the Eucharistic one, the communion at least, *sub specie vini*, must have taken place at the same time at which the fourth cup was drank in the Passover ritual, that is, after the completion of the Hallel, the Great Hallel, and the blessing of the song. From the preliminary information given by St. Luke, as well as from the consecration, we may say so much with confidence, that it is to be placed somewhere between the filling and the partaking of the fourth cup. The ancient Liturgy rests, as we shall afterwards see, upon the supposition that the consecration took place before the last verse but one of the Great Hallel or Ps. cxxxvi., a supposition which we may at once adopt, as no different ground lies before us. The first taking up of the cup and the preliminary statement of its distribution can thus be placed immediately before the consecration of the bread, or before Ps. cxxxvi., or before Ps. cxviii., or lastly, before the second part of the Hallel beginning with Ps. cxv.

The last two conjectures have almost the same probability; for while it appears to lie next to it—this taking up and direction immediately in connection with the filling and mixing of the fourth cup, that is, immediately before the singing of the Hallel—the Christian Liturgy begins the actual proceedings connected with the oblation with the Preface, which, as we shall see, is taken from Ps. cxviii., which seems to indicate that the Saviour must have said or done the Eucharistic celebration as such a beginning before that psalm.

From the representation of the Gospel of St. Luke there follow two weighty conclusions. First, it appears clearly from it that both consecrations took place after the filling of the fourth cup, and it is also extremely probable that they took place immediately together. It has been objected to this, that it is said of the consecration of the bread that it was performed "during supper," while the consecration of the wine took place "after supper." This exegetical argument is, however, inconclusive, on this ground, that both statements as to the time are not placed together in the same account; but St. Matthew and St. Mark only mention the one, and St. Luke and St. Paul only the other. Consequently, the expression "during supper" may have the general meaning, "as they were assembled for the celebration of the Passover Supper," while the fixing of the time of the cup is only given in order to show that it was the fourth cup. In these statements as to the time there is involved no necessity to separate the consecration of the bread from that of the wine, and to place the former within the actual time of the supper, perhaps at the beginning of it, at the ritual breaking and dividing of the unleavened bread, or still earlier, at the words, "This is the bread of misery." The unsuitableness of this last hypothesis, which has been frequently employed for an extremely superficial explanation of the words of institution, cannot be mistaken, for before the conclusion of the Haggada nothing could be eaten except the green herbs, in order apparently to begin the supper, and to lead the children to ask their questions. The first hypothesis could be made in harmony with the Jewish Passover ceremonies, but is equally excluded by the account given by St. Luke, according to which the consecration of the bread could in no way have taken place before the filling of the

The Institution of the Holy Eucharist. 169

fourth cup. Lastly, we can leave out of view the attempt to connect the eucharistic bread with the Asikoman, as in the time of Christ it is known that the Asikoman consisted, not in a piece of bread, but in a piece of the Passover lamb. It is also certain that both consecrations (to use the Jewish terminology) took place over the fourth cup, so that no one certainly could maintain the singular opinion that they were divided at the different parts of the Hallel; and that both consecrations followed each other immediately is therefore exegetically the view that commends itself from dogmatic considerations and the custom of the Church during eighteen centuries, and is the only right one.[49]

But there is still another dogmatic and not unimportant result from the narrative of St. Luke, viz. the certainty that the words of Christ, "Take and eat," as well as the "giving" of the Eucharistic bread, do not imply an immediate communion before the consecration

[49] [It must be confessed that this argument of Professor Bickell is not altogether satisfactory. By identifying the Eucharistic cup with the fourth cup, he places himself under the necessity of placing the consecration of the bread between the third and the fourth cup, that is, after supper; and has thus to explain away the clear inference from St. Luke's statement, and to put a forced construction upon the distinct statement by St. Matthew and St. Mark as to the time of the consecration of the bread, as well as the passage of St. Paul, where he terms the Eucharistic cup the cup of blessing; but it can hardly be said that he has been successful. When St. Luke attaches to the cup the indication of time, that it was "after supper," he clearly implies that the consecration of the bread was during supper, and thus agrees with St. Matthew and St. Mark. Then the expression "during supper," when literally rendered, as in our Revised Version, is "while they were eating." Eating what? It refers back to the previous

of the wine, but a mere announcement of that which the disciples, not immediately, but after the consecration, under both heads were to do. For exactly in the same manner St. Luke informs us that already, before the consecration of the bread, the Saviour had said at first, taking the cup, "Take it and divide it among yourselves,"—words which, as we have seen, in every respect contain only a preliminary direction as to what they afterwards performed. That, however, the evangelists mention the "giving" of the *species pani* before the consecration of the wine, might well occur in the interest of a more convenient and superficial representation, inasmuch as they communicate everything relative to one *species* before they proceed to the other, by which the parallelism between both is more clearly brought forward. An interchange of this arrangement as to the things done at each moment with the actual time when they occurred, was so little

---

verses, as in ver. 17, "Where wilt Thou that we prepare for Thee to eat the Passover?" that is, the Passover lamb. Then ver. 21, "and as they were eating;" and again, ver. 26, "And as they were eating, Jesus took bread," etc. It was therefore the Passover lamb which they were eating, and which the Mischna terms "the body of the Passover;" and then Jesus took bread, and blessed it, and said, "*This is My body. Take, eat,*" etc. There surely can be no doubt as to the exquisite appropriateness of the consecration of the bread as His body while eating the Passover lamb, which prefigured it. Then, if this is the true time, it follows that the third cup, which immediately followed it when the eating was ended, that is, after supper, was the Eucharistic cup. When St. Paul, in the 12th chapter of the Corinthians, calls it the cup of blessing, it is clear from the context that he was addressing the Jewish portion of the community, and every Jew must have understood him to mean the third cup.—Tr.]

The Institution of the Holy Eucharist. 171

to be apprehended, as each Christian knew the latter from the Liturgy, and knew well that the Saviour had actually so proceeded in the institution of the holy Eucharist.

The "blessing" of the bread mentioned in these accounts, as well as the "thanksgiving" over the cup, we hold as identical with the words of consecration, which were verbally pronounced after the end of each sentence, in order not to interrupt the immediate succession of the particular moments, but are shortly indicated before the accordant passage according to the order of time. Moreover, the words of consecration are indicated not only as apparent as following after the before-mentioned acts, for the participle "saying" that preceded them connect them not only with the next, but with all the preceding aorists, and express that these words were only pronounced during each act, or also only during any one of them. Still it is always possible to understand under the terms "blessing" and "thanksgiving" a full Eucharistic prayer in accordance with the Canon, which Christ had uttered at the place from Ps. cxxxvi., so that the words of consecration only expressed a part of the blessing. This seems unlikely on account of the close connection of the old Christian Canon with Ps. cxxxvi.

If, however, under the "blessing" the words of consecration are to be understood, it follows from that that the breaking of bread must have followed its consecration. We venture, however, in regarding the primitive Christian Liturgy, which has hitherto preserved an exact agreement with the solemn institution of the holy Eucharist, to go a little farther, and to accept that it exactly holds good with the "breaking" and with the "blessing," that is, that the breaking took place after the consecration of the wine, and are mentioned merely on account of the more superficial representation after the consecration of the bread.

The breaking of bread by our Lord ought not, as is usually the case, to be confounded with the customary ritual-breaking at the Passover, for the former took place after the supper at the Hallel, the latter at the beginning of the supper-time. The Eucharistic bread especially did not belong to the two, or later three, cakes which came to intercession in the Passover ceremonies, but to that intended for the actual supper. For the ritual cakes were before the destruction of the temple entirely consumed at the beginning of the supper, though in later times, after a half had been kept for the Asikoman, at least before the close of it. In the meanwhile, although the Eucharistic breaking of bread is different from the Jewish ritual-breaking, still a comparison between them may clear up many points. The breaking at the Passover evening was a double one. The first consisted in this, that the cake was divided into two halves, in order to symbolise the misery of the Israelites in the Egyptian servitude; while the second had merely the practical object of breaking off a piece of the bread to be consumed by each guest at the table. The breaking of bread performed by Christ had in every respect the latter object, but very probably the former also, for not only does every Liturgy recognise a symbolic *fractio hostiæ* independent of any relation to the communion, but the words of institution also indicate that there lay in the breaking a symbolic relation to the sufferings of Christ.

We arrange, therefore, the periods of time belonging to the celebration of the institution of the holy Eucharist in the Passover ritual in the following manner:—After the ending of the supper and the thanksgiving prayer, the Saviour apparently then took one of the cakes of bread which remained over, and placed it before Him. Then He filled His cup with wine, mixed it with water, and gave His disciples, either immediately at or before the chanting of Ps. cxviii., the direction that all should take and drink out of this one cup. After He in the usual manner sang the second part of the Hallel (Ps. cxv.–cxviii.), the disciples responding at the proper place, He recited the short prayer which precedes the Hallel blessing, and began then the song of the Great Hallel (Ps. cxxxvi.), the apostles responding at each verse with the refrain. He stopped before the twenty-fifth verse, consecrated first the bread and then the wine, when He finished the Great Hallel, and concluded with the blessing of the song. He then broke the consecrated bread, at first probably symbolically, in two halves, and then in small portions, one of which He gave to each of the disciples for communion. The cup, however, he had passed round the circle, and each drank out of it. We are told by both St. Matthew and St. Mark that Christ and the apostles after singing a hymn left the supper-room. It is, of course, possible that the Hallel was meant by this, but it is very unlikely, because the Hallel must have been finished before the communion. These words are more naturally explained by supposing that after the communion a particular psalm was sung as a thanksgiving. It may have been Ps. xxxiii., "The Lord is my shepherd," which, according to a view presented in the Babylonian Gemara, was wont to be sung after the Hallel, and its expressions could be very appropriately used for a prayer after the communion. It came, then, in place of the blessing of the wine after the fourth cup, which through the consecration had lost its applicability.

§ 2. The Ante-Communion.

Having fixed the position which the consecration and communion occupied in the last Passover supper of Jesus, we may now pass to a coherent comparison of the Jewish ritual with the Christian Liturgy. In doing so, however, we must carefully distinguish between the two constituent parts of which the Liturgy from the beginning consisted. The actual Eucharistic part, or Anaphora, which begins with separation and bringing of the elements, is substantially fulfilled in the consecration and closed with the communion, was from the first preceded by an introduction consisting of lessons from the Bible, chanting of psalms, sermon, prayers, and blessings, which did not strictly belong to the Eucharistic part, but still stood in a greater or less close connection with it, and is here for shortness called the ante-communion. The beginning of it, the lessons interrupted by psalmody, with the sermon, stands in reality in no inward relation to the Eucharistic part. The removal of the catechumens, energumens, and penitents, under certain prayers and blessings, make the celebration of the Eucharist possible, and could only be celebrated in presence of the baptized and those entitled to the communion. But this part did not begin at once, for there were first the prayers of the faithful, which contained the intercessions called for by the deacon for all petitions of the Church, as also the blessing of the faithful by the bishop or priest. These prayers were thus brought into a closer connection with the actual Eucharist. That the priests and again the deacon repeated their contents after the consecration, in order to apply the eucharistic offering for all the persons and petitions mentioned in it, but in the ante-communion they are simply intercessions, and not sacrificial prayers. The *Pax*, which follows the priestly blessing, belongs, lastly, as we shall soon see, in accordance with its origin, equally to the ante-communion; but it was, even at an early period, regarded, according to the prescription of

Christ, as the first preparation for the bringing of the offering, and the Easterns actually begin the Anaphora with it.

The actual Eucharistic proceeding, which extends from the oblation of the elements to the close of the service, is nothing more than the continuation and repetition committed by our Lord to the apostles of what He Himself did and instituted during the Passover supper. Since then the apostles, as already observed, would have adhered, not only to what related to the substance of the words of institution, but also to the whole of the rest of the celebration; to the representation of that consecration and communion celebrated at the fourth Passover cup we might thus expect that the actual eucharistic service would, besides the words of consecration added by Christ Himself, accord in the closest manner with the last portion of the Passover ritual from the filling of the fourth cup to the close of it. There was therefore the less any ground to depart in the Anaphora from the exclusive pattern of the Passover ritual, as the Passover celebration was itself a type of the continued offering of Christ in the holy Eucharist, and as the eucharistic service, according to its meaning, always remains the same without either the necessity of any change or of undergoing any alteration from the influence of the Church's year.

The two grounds above given draw this conclusion along with them, that they represent the ante-communion—that is, the first part consisting of psalmody,

Scripture lessons, and sermon—as variable, so that it cannot be a pattern of the Passover service applicable only to the 14th Nisan. It is true there can be observed in the actual Haggada a distinct resemblance to a sermon in the bidding of the blessing of the table to the prayers of the faithful. Still the resemblance is so general and indefinite that we can better declare the ante-communion to be an especial function for the worship of God, which the apostles obtained elsewhere and prefixed to the actual Eucharistic service as a preparation and introduction. Now, as the Jewish service, with the exception of a repeated reading of the part of the law appointed for Sabbath-morning or Sabbath-evening and Monday and Thursday morning, knew no other varying lessons from the law and the prophets, with the sermon which followed them, than that in the Schacharith or Sabbath-morning prayer, it is a reasonable supposition that the ante-communion beginning with Scripture lessons and a sermon was formed after the model of the last part of the Sabbath-morning prayer from the reading of the Mosaic Parascha to the end, to which must be added the additional prayer Musaph in immediate connection with the Sabbath-morning prayer. A comparison of the particulars will justify the correctness of this supposition. There is nothing, moreover, of any arbitrariness in this that we do not compare the ante-communion with the entire Sabbath-morning prayer, but only with the latter part of it, for it consists of four constituent parts independent of each other, which can be separated from one another, and the authorised time for the performance of each has, according to the Mischna, a different duration, viz. the psalmody, the Schma, the actual prayer or Schmone Esre, and the reading of the Thora, with which Haftara, sermon, and intercession are conjoined, as it is only after the intercession that the Thora is again placed in the ark. We are therefore fully warranted in regarding this last part as a peculiar independent service of God, and paralleling it with the ante-communion. It might rather create a doubt that in this comparison we also avail ourselves of the second Schmone Esre, which on Sabbath was added as the Musaph prayer, for the Musaph could be prayed during the whole day as long as it was light, and the Mincha had not been performed. But in practice the Musaph has always been attached immediately to the end of the morning prayer, so that it represents in a certain degree merely a continuation of it.

Like the last part of the Sabbath-morning prayer, the ante-communion began originally with the reading of a varying portion of the Mosaic law and another out of the prophets. For, according to the second book of the *Apostolical Constitutions*, there must be given at least two Old Testament lessons. The same appears also from the following rubric of the Liturgy of St. James: "Then the sacred words of the Old Covenant and the prophets are fully read, and the incarnation, the sufferings, the resurrection, the ascension, and the glorious second coming of the Son of God is taught." This primitive rubric transplants us at once to the very oldest time, in which no New Testament writings as yet existed; but the apostles and their companions, after reading of the books of Moses (for these are to be understood by the "Old Covenant") and the prophets, preached the gospel to the people on the basis of what they themselves had seen and heard. Still the New Testament lessons were at an early period introduced, and restricted the Old Testament lessons more and more, as this has indeed taken place in the Roman rite. It does not belong to this treatise to enter further into this point, as it concerns itself merely with the relation of the Christian worship to the Jewish, and not with the independent development of the former. It is possible that at a later period many ceremonies used at the reading of the Thora were transferred to the Gospel.

The lessons from Scripture were, according to the second book of the *Apostolical Constitutions*, interrupted by the chanting of psalms, in this manner, that invariably between two lessons, psalms were chanted by the church singers, and, indeed, always one psalm; as the 17th canon of the Council of Laodicea shows, more psalms were not to follow it, but after each psalm a lesson was prescribed. At the end of each psalm the people sang the Antiphon[50] or Aprostich. Moreover,

[50] If I consider a circumstance here conveniently in a note which requires a book for itself, this is done in order to show another example of the origin of the Christian rites from the Jewish, and at the same time, as much as possible, to simplify a very complicated liturgical

the singing of a psalm between the Scripture lessons appears to have first found currency in the Christian Church, for in the Synagogue it was unknown at this place, although much use of psalmody was otherwise problem. The responding is in one place, as also otherwise named ὑπακούειν, a word which in this meaning is merely intelligible as a translation of the Hebrew *anaj*, as this last means both to hear and to answer. For the responsarium we find in St. Methodius the word ὑπακοή, which, moreover both in its origin and in its meaning, exactly corresponds with the expressions used by the Syrian Christians— Unnitha and Enjana. When Tertullian says that they added to the singing of the psalms Hallelujah and "that sort of psalm," he means by "that sort of psalm" short, generally known acclamations, verses of psalms or metrical lines with which the whole people took part in the singing. These responses were sung either first at the end of the entire psalms, like our Antiphon, or they were repeated after one or two verses as in our Invitatorium, the Greek Antiphona, and the Syrian Enjania. This mode of responding we find adopted in the psalms themselves. Thus Ps. cxxvi. was from the first arranged that the refrain, "For Thy mercy endureth for ever," should be sung by the congregation after each verse. In Ps. xlii. and xliii., which were originally connected together, there is a refrain verse at the end of each strophe. The Eastern Christians began, moreover, very early to say after each verse of the psalm a varying instead of a permanent response. By the adoption of this principle on certain parts of the psalm arose the Greek Prokeimena, Stichera, etc.; and the Syrian Kala, by the adoption of the canones from the biblical Cantica. The metrical hymns, too, had these responses, which consisted of one or several verses, and were repeated after every strophe. The Greeks named this responding Hypakoe; the Syrians, Unnitha. With perfect certainty we can point to the one from the time of St. Methodius and to the other from the time of St. Ephraim. But its Jewish origin can be at once certainly established by Philo's account of the Therapeutæ, according to whom they possessed their metrical hymns, whose strophes were constructed according to different kinds of Schemata (plainly after the manner of the Syrian Midrasch and the Greek Troparie). These hymns, some of which could even in the time of Philo be called old, were either sung by two alternate choirs or only by one cantor, while all present united in the response at the close of each strophe.

made. At first, after the conclusion of the intercession, two psalms were sung, during and after the replacing of the Thora in the ark. After the last lesson out of Holy Scripture the sermon was preached; in the Schacharith after the Haftara, in the ante-communion after the Gospel.

What next followed in the primitive Christian ante-communion, viz. the dismissal of the Catechumens, Energumens, and Penitents, arose out of the peculiar relations of the older Church, and can find in the synagogue worship no immediate pattern. It connects itself so closely in contents, form, and arrangement with the immediately following prayer of the faithful, borrowed from the Schacharith and Musaph, that it is plainly to be regarded as an imitation of it, and so at least immediately arises out of the Jewish service; for as the prayer of the faithful consists of a summons by the deacon, of petitions which he prays and to which the kneeling faithful respond, lastly, of the direction by the deacon to stand up and receive with bowed heads the priestly blessing, so in the same manner the catechumens, energumens, and penitents, at the summons of the deacon, kneel while he prays for them, the faithful, exclaiming Kyrie Eleison, raise themselves at his summons and receive with bowed heads the blessing of the priest. These three or four functions, before the removal of those classes excluded from the celebration of the Eucharist, can be regarded as a multiplication of the Litany prayer and blessing of the faithful following it, which arose within the Christian Church, to the comparison of which. with the similar Jewish prayers we now turn.

As already observed, it must not be kept out of view in this comparison that those Litany petitions or collects (by the Greeks called Synapte or Ektene, by the Syrians Proclamations or Katholika) which are recited by the deacon, are not only repeated in shorter form after the Canon, but also, as regards their contents, are throughout identical with the intercessory prayers recited by the priest after the consecration. In order to fix the particular petitions and the order in which they should follow, all three forms must be compared. In doing so, the evidence also of other old Liturgies must be taken in order to determine doubtful points, especially that of the Syrian Liturgy of St. James. From this we learn that the collects began with intercessions for the whole Church militant, and especially for the particular diocese. They then prayed for all faithful bishops, priests, deacons, and clergy; further, for the congregation, and especially for virgins, widows, and orphans, married persons and their children, ascetes, givers of alms, and bringers of oblations, for sick and others oppressed. The intercessions which followed for the emperor, the government, and the army, connected themselves appropriately in the first century with those for enemies and persecutors. For if, according to the eighth book of the *Apostolical Constitutions*, the first collect only prayed for persecutors, it appears from the second book, as already observed, that in it as well as in the intercessory prayer and in the second collect the emperor and empire is prayed for. Then came the commemoration of the Church triumphant and suffering, as first the holy martyrs and saints, after these the dead and the faithful requiring prayers, and the holy Eucharist were remembered. The prayer for the necessary earthly nourishment, for fruitful seasons and a good harvest, formed the conclusion.

It is hardly necessary to remark how exactly these petitions correspond with those closing the Schacharith. Here the cantor prays, there the deacon. Here the people respond to each petition with Amen, there with Kyrie Eleison. But the contents and arrangements are throughout identical. The intercessions in Schacharith begin likewise with a prayer for the Israelitic community both within and beyond the Holy Land, for the president of the people, the heads of the schools, and the scribes. Then the particular congregation and those belonging to it are especially prayed for; for those also who have built synagogues or brought gifts for religious purposes, givers of alms, and workers for the general wellbeing; on some days at least those who voluntarily fast are also prayed for. Then according to the occasion come prayers for lying-in women and their children, as well as for the sick. After the prayer for the king, come, lastly, the remembrance of the martyrs, and the prayers for rest for the souls of deceased adherents.

But where in the Jewish ritual is the prayer for

fruitful seasons? We believe it is to be found in the Schmone Esre of the Musaph, which on Sabbaths is immediately at the close of the Schacharith, at the end of which the intercessions are continued. As already said, the Schmone Esre does not consist on the Sabbath of the eighteen benedictions, but the twelve in the middle are omitted, because sorrows and destitution should not be mentioned on this day; the first three and last three benedictions are alone retained, betwixt which a seventh, appropriate to the Sabbath, was inserted. The second of these prayers praise the power of God, which is shown in the nourishment of all living and the resurrection of the dead. It is true that here rain and fruitfulness is merely mentioned, not prayed for, and so perhaps it is not too bold to regard the ninth benediction as the pattern which prays directly for a fruitful year, rich harvest, and rain. To be sure, this prayer is only used on week-days; but as the Christian Liturgy is intended for every day, it might take in such portions as are omitted on the Sabbath. Those to whom this may appear too arbitrary, may regard as the pattern the prayer which on the Sabbath before the new moon is added as the last intercession after the Haftara; in it a happy and a holy life, sufficient nourishment and riches in the coming month, are prayed for. Then if Rab is mentioned as the compiler of it, this does not exclude the supposition that a similar prayer may have been used at an earlier period, and its present form only have been fixed by Rab.

Before the last prayer of the Schmone Esre, if a priest was present he gives the Aaronitic blessing prescribed by the Thora with uplifted and outstretched hands to the people standing before him with bowed heads. From this blessing the benediction has arisen, which after the conclusion of the collects the bishop or the priest, likewise with outstretched hands (whence the Easterns term such blessings the laying on of hands), pronounces over the people standing then with bowed heads. With this comparison we are in the advantageous position, not only to rest upon internal grounds, however probable, but to produce a primitive testimony for the origin of the one blessing from the other. In the second book of the *Apostolical Constitutions*, cap. 57, is the verbal statement, "Then should the deacon recite a prayer for the entire Church and the whole world, its parts and ends, for the priests and superiors, for the high priest and the emperor, for the peace of all; and then the high priest should bless the people while he entreats for peace for them, as also Moses commanded the priest to bless the people with these words, 'The Lord bless thee and keep thee. The Lord lift up His countenance upon thee, and give thee peace.' The bishop also should pray, and say, 'Save, O Lord, Thy people, and bless their inheritance, whom Thou hast obtained and bought through the precious blood of Thy Christ, and hast called a royal priesthood and a holy people.'" These words are found almost *verbatim* in the Episcopal benediction after the collects which are contained in the eighth book of the *Apostolical Constitutions*. It is, however, much fuller, and a paraphrase of that short blessing given in the second book.

After the Aaronitic blessing the Schmone Esre was concluded with the last petition, "Bestow peace," etc., which entreats for peace, and concludes with the clause, "Praised be Thou, O Lord, that Thou blessest with peace Thy people Israel." This petition, although it accords with the conclusion of the Aaronitic blessing, also accords with the words of the priest in the ante-communion, "The peace of the Lord be with you all;" to which the people respond, "and with thy spirit." After this the clergy and people exchanged the kiss of peace, which was unknown to the Jews, and a peculiarly Christian ceremony, already mentioned by the Apostles Peter and Paul. But as it is connected with the last petition of the Schmone Esre for peace, it belongs properly to the ante-communion; still it was at an early period reckoned to belong to the Anaphora as a symbol of the peacefulness and brotherly love necessary for the eucharistic oblation and communion. The Roman Liturgy alone has misplaced the Pax Domini sit semper vobiscum, and the kiss of peace with its prayer, between the paternoster and the communion. It was so as early as the time of Pope Innocent I., but not in the time of Justin Martyr; and that this, though a reasonable place, cannot be the original one, is shown not only by the unanimous testimony of all other

Liturgies, but likewise by its comparison with the last petition of the Schmone Esre.

While therefore, in the ante-communion, antiphons and responses were said by the congregation, the psalms by the cantors, Scripture lessons by the lectors, Gospel and collects by the deacon, there remained for the priests properly nothing except the benedictions taken from the Aaronitic blessing. Of the functions of the cantors or delegates of the congregation none were imposed upon them that would show distinctly that the New Testament presbyters were actually sacrificial priests like the successors of Aaron, not, however, simple "elders of the Church" or officers of the congregation who had undertaken for its better order the conduct of the worship of God. For the bestowing of the Aaronitic blessing was and is most strictly forbidden to any one not descended from the priestly family. In this it does not stand in opposition that the priest also said the prayer of the kiss of peace which we have identified with the last petition of the Schmone Esre; for, on the one hand, it touches upon the close of the Aaronitic blessing; on the other hand, according to the treatise Berachoth, the priest who gives the blessing could also recite the Schmone Esre, if one knew that he possessed sufficient consideration to give the blessing before the last petition, and after it to return to the last petition.

In order to make the agreement between the Sabbath-morning prayer and the ante-communion still more clear, we close this paragraph with a survey of the two formularies placed opposite each other. The first column contains the Jewish ritual, the second what in the Clementine Liturgy accords with it. The collects must be given in a threefold form, as this Liturgy not only repeats them shortly after the Canon, but their contents are included almost *verbatim* in the intercessory prayer of the priest after the consecration. The parallel parts are, besides being placed opposite each other, also distinguished by similar numbers. The series is throughout that in actual use, only in the intercessions of the collects some unimportant transpositions are made which, from a comparison of these formularies in the Clementine Liturgy, were evidently marked out as necessary.

Close of Jewish Morning Prayer.	Ante-Communion in Clementine Liturgy.
1. Reading of a section out of the Mosaic books (Parascha).	1. Lesson from books of Moses.
2. Reading of a section out of the prophets (Haftara).	2. Lesson from the prophets. Psalm sung between each lesson. Epistle. Gospel.
3. Sermon.	3. Sermon. Prayers and blessings before dismissal of catechumens, energumens, and penitents.

The Ante-Communion.

Jewish Sabbath-Morning Prayer.	1. Clementine Collects.	Clementine Intercessory Prayer.	2. Clementine Collects.
4. From heaven falls to their share grace, favours, mercy, long life, rich support, heavenly help to our lords and teachers, the holy colleagues in the land of Israel and in Babylon, the professors, princes of the exile, academy directors, and judges at the gate, all their scholars, and all disciples of their disciples, and all students in law; the King of the world bless them, prolong their life, multiply their days, give length to their years, and may they be freed and saved from all necessities and misfortunes. The Lord of Heaven be their help at each time and hour, and let us say, Amen.	4. Let us pray for the peace and happy settlement of the world and the holy Churches. R. Kyrie Eleison. Let us pray for the holy Catholic and Apostolic Church, which is spread from one end of the earth to the other. R. Kyrie Eleison. Let us pray for every episcopate which is under the whole heaven, for those that rightly divide the word of truth, that the God of mercy may grant them to continue in His holy Churches in health, honour, and long life, and afford them an honourable old age in godliness and righteousness. R. Kyrie Eleison. And let us pray for our presbyters, that the Lord may deliver them from every unreasonable and wicked action, and afford them a presbyter-	4. We further pray unto Thee, O Lord, for Thy holy Church, spread from one end of the world to the other, for every episcopate who rightly divide the word of truth, for the whole presbytery, for the deacons and all the clergy, that Thou wilt make them wise, and replenish them with the Holy Spirit.	4. Let us pray for this Church and people. Let us pray for every episcopate, every presbytery, all the deacons and ministers in Christ, for the whole congregation, that the Lord will keep and preserve them all. R. Kyrie Eleison.

Jewish Sabbath-Morning Prayer.	1. Clementine Collects.	Clementine Intercessory Prayer.	2. Clementine Collects.
	ate in health and honour. *R.* Kyrie Eleison. Let us pray for all the deacons and ministers of Christ, that the Lord may grant them an unblamable ministration. *R.* Kyrie Eleison. Let us pray for the readers, singers, virgins, widows, and orphans. *R.* Kyrie Eleison.		
5. From heaven there is imparted grace to this whole holy community, to the great with the small, to children and women. The King of the world bless them, and let us say, Amen. He who has blessed our fathers, Abraham, Isaac, and Jacob, bless the whole community, with all other communities, them and their wives, sons and daughters, and all their belongings.	5. Let us pray for this holy diocese. *R.* Kyrie Eleison. Let us pray for those that are in wedlock and in childbearing, that the Lord may have mercy upon them all. *R.* Kyrie Eleison.		5. Let us pray for this Church and the people. *R.* Kyrie Eleison.

6. And those who have set apart houses for places of prayer, and entered them to pray, and have placed candlesticks in them, and given wine for Kiddusch and Habdala, and bread for wanderers and alms for the poor, and all who care truly for the circumstances of the congregation, to them may the Holy One grant the promised reward, and remove from them all sickness, and forgive their sins, and send blessing and prosperity upon every work of their hands, and upon all Israel, their brethren, and let us say, Amen.	6. Let us pray for those that bear fruit in the holy Church, and give alms to the needy, and let us pray for those who offer sacrifices and oblations to the Lord our God, that God, the fountain of all goodness, may recompense them with His heavenly gifts, and give them in this world an hundredfold, and in the world to come life everlasting, and bestow upon them for their temporal things those that are eternal, for earthly things those that are heavenly. R. Kyrie Eleison.	6, 7, 8. We further offer unto Thee for this people, for those that are in virginity and purity, for the widows of the Church, for those in honourable wedlock and childbearing, for the infants of Thy people, that Thou wilt not permit any of us to become castaways.
7. He who has these blessed, let Him bless all those who have bound themselves to fast on Monday and Thursday, and let us say, Amen.	7. Let us pray for the eunuchs who walk holily. Let us pray for those in a state of continence and piety. R. Kyrie Eleison.	
8. He who has blessed, let Him bless the mother (N. N.), with her new-born son (N. N.).	8. Let us be mindful of the infants of the Church, that the Lord may perfect them	

Jewish Sabbath-Morning Prayer.	1. Clementine Collects.	Clementine Intercessory Prayer.	2. Clementine Collects.
May he grow up to the law, and to wedlock, and to good works, and let us say, Amen.	in His fear, and bring them to a complete age. R. Kyrie Eleison.		
9. He who has blessed, may He heal the sick (N. N.), and send him soon perfect health from heaven, as also the other sick in Israel, healing of soul and body, and let us say, Amen.	9. Let us pray for our brethren afflicted with sickness, that the Lord may deliver them from every sickness and every disease, and restore them sound unto Thy holy Church. R. Kyrie Eleison.	9. For those that are sick, that Thou, the helper and assister of all men, will be their support.	
10. He who gave victory to the kings, may He bless, protect, preserve, support, raise, make good, and lift up our celebrated ruler (N. N.). May He give mercy to his heart and the hearts of all his counsellors and commanders, to do good to us, and to all Israel, and let us say, Amen.	10. Let us pray for our enemies, and those that hate us, that the Lord may pacify their anger and scatter their wrath against us. R. Kyrie Eleison.	10. We further pray to Thee, O Lord, for the king and all in authority, for the whole army, that they may be peaceable towards us, that so, leading the whole time of our life in quietness and unanimity, we may glorify Thee through Jesus Christ, who is our hope. We further beseech Thee for those	10. Let us pray for kings and those in authority, that they may be peaceable towards us, that so we may have and lead a quiet and peaceable life in all godliness and honesty. R. Kyrie Eleison.

11. May God remember the souls of my parents, grandparents, uncles and aunts, brethren and sisters, that have gone into eternity. May their souls be embraced in the bundle of life with the souls of Abraham, Isaac, and Jacob, Sara, Rebecca, Rachel, and Leah, and with all other righteous ones in the paradise Eden, and let us say, Amen.

May God remember the souls of all my relations who have been killed, for the sake of the hallowing of His name, and let us say, Amen.

The Father of Mercy bring home in mercy the pious, righteous, and guiltless, the holy host who have given their lives for the hallowing of His name. May God remember them for good, with the other righteous from the beginning of the world.

11. Let us pray for every Christian soul. *R*. Kyrie Eleison.

that hate us and persecute us for Thy name sake, that Thou wilt pacify their anger.

11. We further offer to Thee also for all those holy persons who have pleased Thee from the beginning of the world, patriarchs, prophets, righteous men, apostles, martyrs, confessors, bishops, presbyters, deacons, subdeacons, readers, singers, virgins, widows, and lay persons, with all those whose names Thou knowest.

11. Let us be mindful of the holy martyrs, that we may be thought worthy to be partakers of their trial.

Jewish Sabbath-Morning Prayer.	1. Clementine Collects.	Clementine Intercessory Prayer.	2. Clementine Collects.
12. May it please Thee, our Lord God, and God of our fathers, to renew us this month to good and to blessing, and to give us prosperous life, life of peace and of good, of blessing, and of nourishment, of riches and of honour, life in which the wish of our heart to good shall be fulfilled. *R.* Amen. Bless to us, our Lord God, this year, and all kinds of its fruits for good, and give dew and rain for blessing on the earth, and satisfy us with Thy goodness. Blessed be Thou, O Lord, who blessest the year. *R.* Amen.		12. We further offer to Thee also for the good temperature of the air and the fertility of the fruits, that so, perpetually partaking of the good things derived from Thee, we may praise Thee without ceasing, who gavest food to all flesh.	12. Let us pray for the good temperature of the air and the perfect maturity of the fruits. *R.* Kyrie Eleison.

Jewish Sabbath-Morning Prayer.	Clementine Ante-Communion.
13. Aaronite blessing.	13. Benediction of the priests on the faithful.
14. Give peace over us and Thy whole people Israel. For it is pleasant to Thee to bless Thy people each time and hour with Thy peace. Praised be Thou, O Lord, who blessest Thy people Israel with peace. *R.* Amen.	14. The praise of the Lord be with you all. *R.* And with thy spirit. Kiss of peace.

§ 3. THE CANON OR ANAPHORA.

Under the name of Canon, we here understand, not only that part of the Eucharistic service usually so called, but the entire actual sacrificial service, from the oblation of the elements to its close, in contradistinction to the ante-communion; it is therefore that part of the service which the Easterns called the Anaphora. We have already seen that this part of the Eucharistic service must necessarily connect itself with the last part of the Passover ritual, from the filling of the fourth cup to the end; and this anticipation will be found fully confirmed by the comparison of the Canon with the Hallel in every particular.

The oblation accords with the filling of the fourth cup, which most likely in the celebration of the Institution immediately preceded the preparing of the bread to be consecrated. The mixing of the wine with water arose out of the Passover ritual, according to which each cup must be mixed with water. It is unnecessary to seek in the Eastern Haggada for a pattern of the washing of the hands at the oblation, as the meaning and appropriateness of this ceremony is self-evident. The three washings of the hands in the Passover ritual take place at other parts of it. The oblation, mixing, and washing of hands do not appear to have been originally accompanied by words. Still the priest prayed in secret at the conclusion of them, from which our *Secreta* arose, which at present is separated from the *Dominus vobiscum* and *Oremus*, which belong to it by the later inserted oblation, mixing, and hand-washing prayers. During the presenting of the elements and the silent prayer of the priest, a psalm was probably at all times sung.

After the offertorium begins the Preface. As already observed, we assume that in the apostolic Liturgy the Preface contained only the general thought that praise and thanks on earth, as in heaven, were due to God, while the whole special foundation of these statements first appears in the Canon. Further, that the words borrowed from Ps. cxviii. 25-27 followed from the beginning the *Sanctus*. In the order of the Passover ritual, the Preface corresponds with the second part of the Hallel, or Ps. cxv.–cxviii. But as the Hallel could not suitably be used as the Preface, or serve in relation to the contents as a pattern, there remained no alternative but, on the one hand, to make the Preface resemble the Hallel as much as possible in a more formal relation to it, viz. in the mode of its recitation; on the other hand, to adopt some of the more striking and suitable passages *verbatim* in the Preface. Both, as we shall see, were done. Still they did not apply to the whole Hallel, but only to the last psalm. The reason of this was partly that in this psalm alone passages were found that could be adapted without forcing to this part of the Eucharistic service, partly that it was only in this psalm that responses appeared, while the other Hallel psalms were recited in a quite symmetrical manner; perhaps also that the Saviour paused before the beginning of Ps. cxviii., and gave the advice recorded by St. Luke.

The original responding in this psalm consisted in this, as already remarked, that of the first four verses the reciter sang always the first half of the verse and the congregation the refrain, "For Thy mercy endureth for ever." Further, that in ver. 24 the congregation repeated both halves of the verse after the cantor had recited them; lastly, that in ver. 25 the cantor said only, "Blessed is He that cometh," and "We have blessed you," the congregation, however, responding with the words, "in the name of the Lord" and "out of the house of the Lord." At a later period all the verses from ver. 20 to the end were repeated; but this was not properly responding, it was only that each single verse was in the usual manner twice recited; that is, the cantor recited alone each verse twice, and those present accompanied him both times in a low voice.

We find, then, that it is precisely those passages to which responses were made that are taken into the Preface. Its beginning corresponds with the beginning of the 118th Psalm, partly formally, as both consist of a responding between the liturgist and the congregation; partly materially, as both contain a demand to giving of thanks and praising God, along with the declaration that it is right and our bounden duty. The "Give thanks unto the Lord; for He is good: because His mercy endureth for ever," exactly corresponds with the *Gratias agamus Domino Deo nostro* and the *Dignum et justum est*. The apostles preceded it by two other responses, viz. the Pauline blessing (2 Cor. xiii. 13) and the *Sursum corda;* while the Preface itself joined to the last the response to the opening verse of our psalm with the *vere dignum*.

In the Sanctus which closes the Preface we also find the response towards the end of the 118th Psalm, and that again *verbatim*, at least the double Hosanna (a word that only occurs in this particular place in the whole of the Old Testament) and the *Benedictus qui venit in nomine, Domini*, originally probably also, as we have shown in the first part, the words of the verse which follows *Deus Dominus et illuxit nobis*. The formal agreement is thus also preserved, that the Sanctus and Benedictus were sung by the whole people, while the Preface itself was recited only by the priest, in the East silently, but in the West with singing.

Both the beginning and the end of the Preface thus connect themselves closely with Ps. cxviii. On the other hand, a similar connection for the middle of the Preface from the contents of the psalm was made impossible. For the fundamental thought of the Preface—1st, it is our bounden duty to give God praise and thanks; 2nd, therefore with the heavenly host we cry out the three times Holy—other patterns in the Jewish *cultus* must be sought out. The first thought merely sets forth, indeed, the summons of the first four verses. Its further development, however, was taken from the prayer which immediately follows Ps. cxviii., "Thou shouldst be praised;" partly, however, also from the blessing of the song which closes the Great Hallel, as well as from the closing words of the Haggada, "Therefore are we bound," etc. The second thought connects itself, on the other hand, with a prayer which is not to be found in the Passover ritual, but in the Schmone Esre, where it is inserted before the third benediction on the holiness of God. This is in the second part of the Keduscha, which we have already noticed, in which the cantor summons to praise God along with the seraphim, and the congregation join in the three times Holy. How closely the Keduscha agrees with the close of the Preface and the beginning of the Sanctus, both as regards its contents as well as the manner of its recitation, requires no further exposition.

On the other hand, it will be necessary to make some

explanatory remarks as to how it is possible that in one part of the Preface the exact agreement with the order of the Jewish ritual, which we have hitherto found to be so strictly observed in the Christian Liturgy, appears in this instance to be abandoned. This, however, cannot at least be maintained in so far as regards the first fundamental conception of the Preface. It interrupts in no way the accordant order in which the parts follow in the Passover ritual, as it is, in fact, only a further development of the four opening verses of the 118th Psalm. That this further development connects itself in expression in part with other passages of the Passover ritual is quite inconsiderable; for the most significant expressions are taken directly from the prayer which follows Ps. cxviii. But the using the Keduscha in order to express the second fundamental idea of the Preface can, besides the suitableness of its contents, be explained by a more formal ground. The Benedictus taken from Ps. cxviii. 25 has, in fact, a great resemblance to the second response of the congregation in the Keduscha. It lay, therefore, very near to prefix to it this first, the response containing the seraphic hymn, and to use the introductory summons of the cantor as the close of the Preface. The Clementine Liturgy has therefore a double *Benedictus;* that taken *verbatim* from Ps. cxviii. comes first before the communion in the response to the *Sancta Sanctis,* while the short *Benedictus in Secula Amen* after the Sanctus occasioned, indeed, by

Ps. cxvii. 25, but is made similar to the second and third responses of the Keduscha.

After the Hallel there follows in the Passover ritual the Great Hallel, under which designation the Jewish practice, notwithstanding the somewhat different views of some rabbinical writers, preserved in both the Gemaras, was always understood to be the 136th Psalm. This psalm proves the statement that it is our bounden duty to give praise and thanks to God, in that it gives the grounds for it from the Being of God in Himself, from His work of creation, and from the saving and redeeming acts of God in His chosen people. The primitive Christian Canon, however, contains exactly the same expressions, and, indeed, in the same order, perhaps even in the same words, so that it is absolutely impossible to deny a connection between them.

The beginning of the Canon agrees with the first verse of the psalm, which connects it with the Sanctus in all Liturgies except the Roman with the words, "Yes, Thou art in truth holy, and worthy of praise," or with similar doxologic expressions. The second and third verses show the praiseworthiness of God in particular, and glorify Him for what He is in and for Himself as the highest absolute Being. The Canon of the Clementine Liturgy proceeds also with the same thought. The often noticed primitive Syrian Anaphora designates God at this point, in verbal agreement with the psalm, as the Lord of lords. Ver. 4 depicts the passing over from glorifying the Divine Being, as in

Himself perfectly blessed, to the wonderful work of creation undertaken through love. We find this passing over much more fully handled in the Clementine Canon and the old Syrian Anaphora, which last especially lays stress upon the unity of God before the universe was. Vers. 5-9 contain praises for the creation of the world, in particular, viz., the heavens, the earth, the sun, and the moon. The Clementine Liturgy follows throughout in almost verbal agreement, but treats of the works of creation not mentioned in the psalm with equal fulness.[51] It is especially to be brought forward that the remark, on ver. 5, "God has in His wisdom made the heavens," the old Liturgy has allowed itself to speak in a fuller manner of the creation as by His Divine Son. After ver. 9 the Clementine Liturgy, as it lay in its plan to go through the entire redemption decree, inserts a long episode which is not in the psalm, and mentions the creation of man, the command given to him, and the different attitude of God towards His obedient and disobedient descendants, which last is illustrated by examples out of the Old Testament history. From this point the 136th Psalm runs again parallel with the Canon; for what vers. 10-22 say about the punishment of the Egyptians and Canaanites, and about the gracious leading of the people of Israel

---

[51] Perhaps it is not accidental that the Clementine Liturgy in describing the works of creation not mentioned in Ps. cxxxvi., appears to refer to those in Ps. cxxxv., especially to vers. 6 and 7, for this psalm was at an earlier period reckoned by many to belong to the Great Hallel.

in their exodus from Egypt, about their passage through the Red Sea and the wilderness, and, lastly, in their conquest and possession of the promised land, will be found equally in the primitive Christian Liturgy. The circumstance is decisive, that both psalm and Canon carry on the Old Testament history merely to the possession of the land of Canaan, and both break off at precisely the same place. Vers. 23, 24 praise God for redemption. In accordance with this, there is in the Canon mention of the redemptive work of Christ, His life and His sufferings, which depicts the passing over to the account of the institution of the holy Eucharist and the words of consecration. It is of importance to establish here that, according to almost all commentaries, the redemption mentioned in vers. 23, 24 is different from that from Egypt before described.

After the 24th verse our Lord most probably effected the consecration, and directed the apostles to continue the Eucharist which He had instituted. On this account the words of consecration were regarded from the beginning, as their repetition in the First Epistle of St. Paul to the Corinthians shows, to be the substantial, unalterable fundamental portion of the Liturgy.

The words of Christ, "Do this in remembrance of me," only mean, indeed, that the apostles should further celebrate the holy Eucharist, according to the institution of Christ, as a commemoration, continuation, and application of the sacrifice on the cross, and likewise that the remembrance of His sufferings were renewed at and for Him by the eucharistic celebration; still St. Paul draws from these words the conclusion that in the Eucharist the death of our Lord must also be shown forth by distinct words. There is therefore to be found in all Liturgies immediately after the words of consecration a remembrance of the sufferings, the resurrection, the ascension, and the second coming of our Lord.

After the conclusion of the consecration the Saviour recited next the last two verses of the Great Hallel. The former is, "Who giveth food to all flesh: for His mercy endureth for ever." In the Liturgy this verse was applied to the Eucharistic bread, and that in two ways, in so far as, on the one part, the sacrificial and propitiatory, on the other, the sacramental character of the Eucharist, was regarded. For God has given the holy Eucharist to men as well on that account, that it should be brought to Him as the only perfect acceptable oblation, and thus grace and salvation should be attained by all; but also on this account, that all the faithful should receive in it the food of eternal life. In the first view, the verse of our psalm is paraphrased in the offering of the holy body and blood immediately following the remembrance of the sufferings and glorification of Christ, so also through the intercessory prayer, which applies the eternal value of this offering in particular for all men and all officers of the Church. The petitions of the intercessory prayer, as well as the collects recited by the deacon immediately after, are, as already remarked, formed on the model of those already said in the collects of the ante-communion. These last close in a remarkable manner the petition of the Clementine intercessory prayer, relative to the blessing of the harvest, with the verse of our psalm, "who giveth food to all flesh." In so far, on the other hand, as the holy Eucharist is regarded, not as an oblation, but as communion, we find a paraphrase of the same verse in the Epiklesis, which prays God to send His Holy Spirit that He may exhibit the Eucharist as the body and blood of Christ, and thus the communicants receive by it forgiveness of their sins, sanctification, and eternal life. Both modes of regarding it are sharply separated in the East Syrian Liturgies, which place the intercessory prayer after the offering of the holy Eucharist, and pray for the sending of the Holy Spirit only after its conclusion, to which there the usual preparatory prayers for the communion are found. According to the other Liturgies, on the other hand, both modes of viewing it are mixed up together, as the Epiklesis follows the oblation and precedes the intercessory prayer. At all events the Epiklesis relates directly to the communion, as we shall show more fully in the last paragraph.

The last verse of the Great Hallel, "O give thanks unto the God of heaven : for His mercy endureth for ever," corresponds with the close of the Canon, which contains a thankful praise of the Triune God. Its expressions correspond entirely with the order of the Passover ritual taken from the blessing of the song which follows the Great Hallel. To the doxologic conclusion of the Canon the people always responded with Amen. This corresponds with the Amen said by those present at the close of the blessing of the song, as, indeed, it must generally in the Jewish ritual be responded to each benediction. That this custom had been adopted by the apostles in the Christian Church, St. Paul shows in the clearest manner (1 Cor. xiv. 16).

After the conclusion of the Canon and the breaking of the bread, the priest gave again the salutation of peace, and says a blessing prayer preparatory to the communion, which, independently of its special purpose, is equally a multiplication of the benediction after the first collect, which took its rise from the Aaronitic blessing. Upon this follows the *Sancta Sanctis*, with the responses of the people and the communion, during which a psalm was sung. Of all this, the breaking of bread (as the Eucharist is consequently usually called in the New Testament) and the communion has already been examined in reference to the institution of the holy Eucharist. As the fourth cup was drunk immediately after the blessing of the song, it is probable that Christ did not insert any further rite or prayer after it, but immediately broke the bread and gave His body and blood to the disciples. It follows of itself that the usual blessing of the fruit of the vine was omitted before partaking of the holy blood.

On the same ground the usual blessing of the land of

Israel and the fruit of the vine, after partaking of the fourth cup, would be omitted at the celebration of the institution. St. Matthew and St. Mark seem to say that Christ and His disciples replaced it by singing a psalm that might well represent a thanksgiving for the communion, and, according to a reasonable conjecture, was probably the 23rd Psalm.[52] This thanksgiving

---

[52] At all events, by the hymn sung, as noticed by the evangelists, after which our Lord and His disciples left the room, we are to understand the singing of a psalm, and not of other or even extempore songs, as the Manichæan *Umzüge der Apostel* give out. This lying work, already mentioned by Innocent I. and St. Augustine, and described in the *Myriobiblon* of Photius, is, of course, of no historical value; still in the interest of completeness its narrative as to that hymn may find a place here. As the iconoclastic ruling bishops of the pseudo-Council of Constantinople had derived a proof against the holy pictures out of this work, the seventh Œcumenical Council had several sections of this work read in order to show its Manichæan origin, among them the following passage ascribed to the evangelist St. John: "Before Jesus was seized by the mad Jews, acting under the command of the godless serpent, He assembled us all and said, Before I shall be delivered over to them, let us sing a hymn to the Father, and then go out to what stands before us. Then He commanded us to take hands and form a circle; He, however, standing in the middle said, Respond to us with Amen. Then He began to sing and to say, Glory be to Thee, O Father; and we in the circle responded, Amen. Glory be to Thee, O Word; Glory be to Thee, O Grace, Amen. Glory be to Thee, O Spirit; Glory be to Thee, O Holy One; Glory be to Thee, the Glory, Amen. We praise Thee, O Father; we give Thee thanks, O Light, in whom no darkness dwells, Amen. Therefore do we give thanks. I will say, I will be saved and will save, Amen. I will be redeemed and will redeem, Amen. I will be wounded and will wound, Amen. I will be born and give birth; I will destroy and be destroyed, Amen. I will hear and be heard, Amen. I will be understood, who am entirely reason, Amen. I will be washed and will wash, Amen. Grace wings the choir; I will play the flute; Dance all of you, Amen. I will be mourned, complain all of you, Amen." Upon this then

psalm, which closed the celebration of the institution, accords with a thanksgiving prayer of the priest introduced by a summons from the deacon in the Clementine Liturgy, out of which our post-communion has been developed. On this followed one of the frequently repeated benedictions taken from the Aaronitic blessing, and the dismissal of the people by the deacon.

We close this paragraph also with a comparative table placing the primitive Christian Anaphora opposite the last portion of the Passover ritual or the blessing of the Hallel cup, bringing, however, along with it in the Passover ritual those additions and modifications which must enter into the celebration of the institution of the holy Eucharist, partly according to the distinct testimony of the New Testament authorities, partly from the nature of the thing itself.

follows several responses, which, however, do not appear in the Acts of the Council. After the ending of the song the pseudo-St. John proceeds, "After the Lord had ended the choir song with us, He went out."

Close of the Passover Ritual.	Clementine Liturgy.
15. The placing of the bread and the filling of the Hallel cup.	15. Oblation of bread and wine and water.
16. Filling the cup with wine and water. Direction to the disciples later, all to drink out of this one cup.	16. Mixing the wine with water. Washing of hands. Silent prayer of the priest. Paulinian blessing, with response— Lift up your minds. We lift them up to the Lord.
17. Hallel Ps. cxviii. 1. O give thanks unto the Lord; for He is good: R. Because His mercy endureth for ever. 2. Let Israel now say, R. That His mercy endureth for ever. 3. Let the house of Aaron now say, that His mercy endureth for ever. 4. Let them now that fear the Lord say, that His mercy endureth for ever.	17. Let us give thanks to the Lord. R. It is meet and right so to do.

Passover Ritual.	Clementine Liturgy.
18. O Lord our God, let all Thy works praise Thee, and Thy saints, and the righteous ones that do Thy will, and Thy people, the house of Israel, all of them shouting. Let them praise, and bless, and magnify, and glorify, and say out the name of Thy glory with honour and renown, for remembrance of Thy kingdom; for it is good to praise Thee, and also lovely to sing unto Thy name. For ever and ever Thou art God.	18. It is very meet and right before all things to sing a hymn to Thee, who art the true God, who art before all beings.

Passover Ritual.	Clementine Liturgy.
19. We will hallow Thy name on earth as it is hallowed in the highest heavens, as is written by Thy prophet that one called to another and said,	19. For all these things, glory be to Thee, O Lord Almighty. Thee do the innumerable host of angels, archangels, thrones, dominions, principalities, authorities, and powers, Thine everlasting armies adore. The cherubim and six-winged seraphim, with twain covering their feet, with twain their heads, with twain flying, say together, with thousand thousands of archangels, and ten thousand times ten thousands of angels, incessantly as with constant and loud voice,
20. *R.* Holy, holy, holy is the Lord of Sabaoth ; the whole earth is full of His glory. Antiphonally they say, Praised be He. *R.* Praised be the glory of the Lord from their places. And in the Holy Scriptures it is also written, The Lord reigns for ever, the God of Zion, from generation to generation. Hallelujah.	20. Holy, holy, holy, Lord of Hosts, heaven and earth are full of Thy glory. Be Thou blessed for ever. Amen.
21. Hallel Ps. cxviii. 25. O Lord ! Hosanna. *R.* O Lord ! Hosanna. O Lord, send now prosperity. Blessed be He that cometh *R.* In the name of the Lord : we have blessed you *R.* Out of the house of the Lord. God is the Lord, which hath showed us light.	21. Hosanna to the Son of David. Blessed be He that cometh in the name of the Lord, being the Lord God who appeared to us. Hosanna in the highest.
22. Great Hallel. O give thanks unto the Lord ; for He is good : *R.* For His mercy endureth for ever.	22. For Thou art truly holy, and most holy, the highest and most highly exalted for ever.

Passover Ritual.	Clementine Liturgy.
23. O give thanks unto the God of gods : R. For His mercy endureth for ever. O give thanks to the Lord of lords : R. For His mercy endureth for ever.	23. Who art before all beings, from whom the whole family in heaven and earth is named, who only art unbegotten and without beginning, and without a ruler and without a master, who standeth in need of nothing, who art the bestower of everything that is good, who art always and immutably the same.
24. To Him alone who doeth great wonders : R. For His mercy endureth for ever. To Him that by wisdom made the heavens : R. For His mercy endureth for ever.	24. From whom all things came into being as from their proper original. For Thou art eternal knowledge, everlasting sight, unbegotten hearing, untaught wisdom, the first by nature and the manner of being, and beyond all number ; who didst bring all things out of nothing into being by Thy only-begotten Son, but didst beget Him before all ages by Thy will, Thy power, and Thy goodness, without any instrument, the only-begotten Son, God the word, the living wisdom, the first-born of every creature. God and Father of Thy only-begotten Son, who by Thee didst make, before all things, the cherubim and the seraphim, the æons and hosts, the powers and authorities, the archangels and angels ; and after all these didst by Him make this visible world, and all things that are therein. For Thou art He who didst frame the heaven in an arch, and stretch it out like the covering for a tent.
25. To Him that stretched out the earth above the waters :	25. And has founded the earth upon nothing through His sole will.

Passover Ritual.	Clementine Liturgy.
26. To Him that made great lights—the sun to rule by day, the moon and stars to rule by night:	26. Who has fixed the firmament, prepared day and night, brought forth light out of Thy treasures, and on its departure didst bring on darkness for the rest of the living creatures that move up and down in the world, who didst appoint the sun in heaven to rule over the day, and the moon to rule over the night, and didst inscribe in heaven the choir of stars to praise Thy glorious majesty.
27. To Him that smote Egypt in their first-born, And brought out Israel from among them, With a strong hand, and an outstretched arm: To Him that divided the Red Sea into parts, And made Israel to pass through in the midst of it; And overthrew Pharaoh and his host in the Red Sea:	27. Thou, O Lord, didst not overlook the Hebrews when they were afflicted by the Egyptians. Thou didst punish the Egyptians with a judgment of ten plagues, and didst divide the sea and bring the Israelites through it, and drown and destroy the Egyptians who pursued after them.
28. To Him that led His people through the wilderness:	28. Thou didst sweeten the bitter water with wood. Thou didst bring water out of the rock of stone. Thou didst rain manna from heaven, and quails as meat out of the air. Thou didst afford them a pillar of fire by night to give them light, and a pillar of a cloud by day to overshadow them from the heat.
29. To Him which smote great kings, and slew famous kings: Sihon, king of the Amorites; and Og, king of Bashan; and gave their land for an heritage, even an heritage unto Israel His servant:	29. Thou didst declare Joshua to be the general of the army, and didst overthrow the seven nations of Canaan by him. Thou didst divide Jordan, and dry up the rivers of Ethan. Thou didst overthrow walls without instruments or the hand of man.

The Canon or Anaphora.

Passover Ritual.	Clementine Liturgy.
30. Who remembered us in our low estate: *R.* For His mercy endureth for ever. And hath redeemed us from our enemies: *R.* For His mercy endureth for ever.	30. Holy also is Thy only-begotten Son, our Lord and God, Jesus Christ, who in all things ministered to His God and Father, both in Thy various creation and Thy suitable providence, and hast not overlooked lost mankind, and being just ready to perish universally He was pleased by Thy goodwill to become man, who was man's Creator. And He appeased Thee, His God and Father, and reconciled Thee to the world, and freed all these from the wrath to come. He lived bodily, and taught according to the law. He drove away every sickness and every disease from man, and wrought signs and wonders among the people. He manifested His name to those who knew it not. He drove away ignorance. He revived piety and fulfilled Thy will. He finished the work which Thou gavest Him to do. He that was the Judge was judged, and He that was the Saviour was condemned. He that was impassible was nailed to the cross, and He who was by nature immortal died, and He that is the giver of life was buried, that He might loose those for whose sake He came from suffering and death, and might break the bonds of the devil, and deliver mankind from his deceit. Being mindful, therefore, of those things that He endured for our sakes, we give Thee thanks, O God Almighty, not in such manner as we ought, but as we are able, and fulfil His constitution.

Passover Ritual.	Clementine Liturgy.
31. Taking the bread— Take, eat: this My body that is broken for you. Do this in remembrance of Me.	31. For in the same night that He was betrayed, He took bread in His holy and undefiled hands, and looking up to Thee, His God and Father, He brake it, and gave it to His disciples, saying, This is the mystery of the New Covenant, take of it and eat; this is My body, which is broken for many, for the remission of sins.
32. Taking the cup— Drink ye all of this. This cup is the New Covenant in My blood which is shed for many.	32. In like manner also He took the cup, and mixed it of wine and water, and sanctified it, and delivered it to them, saying, Drink ye all of this; for this is My blood, which is shed for many, for the remission of sins.
33. Do this, as oft as ye drink it, in remembrance of Me. For as oft as ye eat this bread, and drink this cup, ye show forth the Lord's death till He come.	33. Do this in remembrance of Me. For as often as ye eat this bread, and drink this cup, ye do show forth My death till I come. Being mindful, therefore, of His passion and death, and resurrection from the dead, and return into heaven, and His future second appearing.
34. Who giveth food to all flesh: R. For His mercy endureth for ever.	34. Offering up of the body and blood of Christ. Invocation of the Holy Spirit for the blessed effect of the communion. The offering of the Eucharistic sacrifice for all men, and
35. O give thanks unto the God of heaven: R. For His mercy endureth for ever. For to Thee is due, O Lord our God, and the God of our fathers, songs, praise, glory, song, might, lordship,	35. For to Thee belongs all glory and worship, and thanksgiving, honour, and adoration, the Father with the Son, and to the Holy Ghost, both now and always, and for everlasting and endless ages for ever. And let all the people say, Amen.

Passover Ritual.	Clementine Liturgy.
honour, greatness, highness, praising, glorifying, hallowing, kingdom, blessing, and thanksgiving, now and for ever. *R.* Amen.	
36. Breaking bread and communion.	36. Breaking of bread and communion.
37. Thanksgiving psalm.	37. Thanksgiving prayer, blessing.

§ 4. Dogmatic Conclusions.

The comparison which we have now concluded has shown that the oldest Christian Liturgy as it is presented to us in the *Apostolical Constitutions*, with the exception of the words of consecration, is closely connected throughout with the Jewish ritual, and likewise the ante-communion with the close of the Sabbath-morning prayer, the Canon, however, with the Hallel recited over the fourth Passover cup. The fact of the decided dependence of the ritual of the Christian Lord's Supper on Jewish patterns renders its establishment through the apostles more than probable, who themselves belonged to the Israelitish people, with whom formularies of divine worship were completely at home; while in the next post-apostolic time the Jewish national element formed only a proportionately slender fragmentary part of Christianity, and, in consequence of the spread of heresies among the Jewish Christians after the destruction of Jerusalem, lost all influence. We find, indeed, already in some of the Apostolic Fathers a so decided opposition to any dependence on Jewish religious customs, that one can hardly believe that in their times the Jewish ritual was first made use of in so extended a manner for the Christian *cultus*. The compilers of the Epistle of St. Barnabas and the Epistle to Diognetus allowed themselves to be drawn into the error that God intended the Mosaic ceremonial law as pure allegory, and that its actual observance was a blamable misunderstanding of the Jews.

Still less to be rejected is the apostolic compilation of the Liturgy, from the circumstance that this close adherence to Jewish patterns in all dioceses of Christendom is found in precisely the same form. For, as we have seen in the first part, there existed during the first three centuries in the whole Church, with some inconsiderable local varieties, one and the same form of celebrating the Lord's Supper, which entirely agrees with that preserved to us in the *Apostolical Constitutions*. If this Liturgy had first arisen in post-apostolic times, it would remain not only inexplicable how in these numerous dioceses, whose clergy and people had no connection with Judaism, and no knowledge of their religious customs, they should yet have regulated their divine service according to the pattern of the Schacharith and the Passover ritual, but also how they could by accident in every diocese have made use of the same Jewish pattern, and exactly in the same manner. Such a miracle of chance is simply impossible. The only satisfactory explanation of this appearance is this, that the apostles, while they were still united together in Jerusalem, had either expressed the Liturgy in writing, or at least established it orally in exact forms, and that each of them had later delivered the same established Liturgy in those districts in which he promulgated the gospel.

The apostolic origin of our Liturgy is, however, brought to complete certainty by the exact accordance of the old Canon of the Mass with the Hallel of the Passover ritual. As agreement can only be brought out by the ceremony of consecration, in which the Passover and the Eucharist are connected together, the fourth Passover cup would be consecrated, and therefore the words of consecration must have been inserted in the Hallel to be recited over it. So can it only be explained by the immediate and still living recollections of the apostles of that first Eucharistic celebration which Christ Himself celebrated with them on that evening of the 14th Nisan. The entire agreement of the Canon with the Hallel cannot absolutely be disputed, but can only without difficulty arise because the apostles so celebrated the Eucharist from the beginning, as the Saviour had shown them from His own example. Any other explanation would lead us to the absurd conclusion that they had originally another mode of celebrating the Lord's Supper, but had later, from a sort of antiquarian feeling, set it aside and substituted first one which agreed with the Hallel, in order by this means to preserve the connection in the consecration ceremony between the Passover and the Eucharist,—a presumption so unhistorical and senseless that it could hardly find a defender. If this use of the Passover ritual was first made in post-apostolic times, the existing component parts of the Liturgy could hardly have been inserted in precisely the same places in which, as we have seen, they must have been adopted by Christ Himself in that Passover eve. Finally, the erroneous and still prevailing opinion in the Greek Church was already widely spread in the second century, that Christ had instituted the holy Eucharist on the 13th Nisan, independently of any connection with the Passover feast,—an opinion which would have made it impossible to have formed the celebration of the Eucharist on the model of that of the Passover ritual.

There are still a few words to be said regarding the invocation of the Holy Spirit. It is difficult to understand how so great a difficulty has been made about a quite simple matter. For when its form in the Clementine Liturgy is regarded with candour, it is quite evident that in it at least the Epiklesis has no relation to the consecration. For here the Holy Spirit is not invited to change the elements into the body and blood of Christ, but "to exhibit them as such." The elements, indeed, represent the body and blood of Christ, but do not enter as such in the exhibition of them to the communicants. Should such words have effected the consecration, the Holy Spirit would have been prayed to do what did not follow. What is really meant appears from the next sentence, according to which, through the operation of the Holy Spirit, forgiveness of sins and sanctification of the communicant should be effected. The Epiklesis stands in the same close connection with the communion which the intercessory prayer does with the consecration, and prays for the influence of the Holy Spirit as the bestower of grace on the recipients of the holy Eucharist, that they should by it be made holy, and thus the real presence of Christ in the sacrament, which is only recognised by the faithful, should by its operation be made evident to unbelievers. That the operation of the Holy Spirit prayed for was originally framed, not to "make the body and blood," but to exhibit or declare it, is shown not only in the Clementine Liturgy, but also by St. Irenæus. In the later Liturgies of the Eastern Church, the Epiklesis appears to have obtained a closer relation to the consecration, without any doubt having arisen as to the exclusive effecting of the consecration by the words of institution. It was only when the great schism arose that, with the hardly-concealed object of increasing the points of difference with Rome, a consecrating power totally unknown to Christian antiquity was given to the Epiklesis. To explain the Epiklesis of the later Liturgies in a satisfactory manner would lead us too far. Suffice it to say, that in the primitive Clementine Liturgy it has a perfectly unexceptionable form.

T. and T. Clark's Publications.

Just published, in post 8vo, price 12s.,

AN INTRODUCTION TO THE LITERATURE OF THE OLD TESTAMENT.

BY

S. R. DRIVER, D.D.,

REGIUS PROFESSOR OF HEBREW, AND CANON OF CHRIST CHURCH, OXFORD;
FORMERLY FELLOW OF NEW COLLEGE, OXFORD.

'Of the plentiful first-fruits of the present publishing season, perhaps the most important is Professor Driver's long-expected "Introduction to the Old Testament." It has been a reproach to modern English theological scholarship that it has produced no authoritative work on the Old Testament as a whole. That reproach is now wiped away, for the book before us will take rank at once with the finest contributions to theological science.'— *The Independent.*

'A book of the first importance.'—*The Bookman.*

Just published, in demy 8vo, price 12s.,

THE EARLY CHURCH:
A HISTORY OF CHRISTIANITY IN THE FIRST SIX CENTURIES.

BY THE LATE

Professor DAVID DUFF, D.D., LL.D., Edinburgh.

Edited by his Son,

DAVID DUFF, M.A., B.D.

Just published, in demy 8vo, price 10s. 6d.,

THE APOLOGY OF THE CHRISTIAN RELIGION.
HISTORICALLY REGARDED WITH REFERENCE TO SUPERNATURAL REVELATION AND REDEMPTION.

BY

Rev. JAMES MACGREGOR, D.D., Oamaru;
SOMETIME PROFESSOR OF SYSTEMATIC THEOLOGY IN THE NEW COLLEGE, EDINBURGH.

T. and T. Clark's Publications.

WORKS BY PROFESSOR DELITZSCH.

Now complete, in Two Vols. 8vo, price 21s.,

A NEW COMMENTARY ON GENESIS.

NOTE.—While preparing the translation, the translator was favoured by Professor Delitzsch with such numerous improvements and additions, that it may be regarded as made from a revised version of the New Commentary on Genesis.

'Thirty-five years have elapsed since Professor Delitzsch's Commentary on Genesis first appeared; fifteen years since the fourth edition was published in 1872. Ever in the van of historical and philological research, the venerable author now comes forward with another fresh edition, in which he incorporates what fifteen years have achieved for illustration and criticism of the text of Genesis. . . . We congratulate Prof. Delitzsch on this new edition, and trust that it may appear before long in an English dress. By it, not less than by his other Commentaries, he has earned the gratitude of every lover of biblical science, and we shall be surprised if, in the future, many do not acknowledge that they have found in it a welcome help and guide.'—Professor S. R. DRIVER in *The Academy*.

'We wish it were in our power to follow in detail the contents of Dr. Delitzsch's most interesting introduction, and to give specimens of the admirable, concise, and lucid notes in his exposition; but we have said enough to show our readers our high estimate of the value of the work.'—*Church Bells*.

'The work of a reverent mind and a sincere believer; and not seldom there are touches of great beauty and of spiritual insight in it.'—*Guardian*.

Just published, in Two Vols. 8vo, price 21s.,

BIBLICAL COMMENTARY ON THE PROPHECIES OF ISAIAH.

With an Introduction by Professor S. R. DRIVER, D.D., Oxford.

NOTE.—By special arrangement with the author, Messrs. CLARK secured the sole right of translation of this Fourth (*and last*) Edition of his 'Isaiah.' It is dedicated to Professors Cheyne and Driver of Oxford. In his Preface the author states that this Fourth Edition contains the fruit of his continued labour, and that a thorough revisal of the whole work has been made.

Canon CHEYNE says:—'Students of Isaiah will greet so early a translation of Delitzsch's "Isaiah." . . . Prefixed to it is an interesting critical sketch by Professor Driver, which will be a useful guide to students, not only of this, but of the other works of the accomplished author.'

'Delitzsch's last gift to the Christian Church. . . . In our opinion, those who would enter into the meaning of that Spirit as He spake long ago by Isaiah, words of comfort and hope which have not lost their significance to-day, cannot find a better guide; one more marked by learning, reverence, and insight, than Franz Delitzsch.'—Professor W. T. DAVISON in *The Expository Times*.

'Commentaries in Europe are not often republished after their author's death, whatever is of permanent value in them being appropriated by their successors. But it may be long before one undertakes the task of expounding the Prophets possessing so many gifts and employing them so well.'—*Guardian*.

T. and T. Clark's Publications.

WORKS BY PROFESSOR C. A. BRIGGS, D.D.

In One Volume, post 8vo, price 7s. 6d.,

MESSIANIC PROPHECY.

By Professor C. A. BRIGGS, D.D.,

EDWARD ROBINSON PROFESSOR OF BIBLICAL THEOLOGY, UNION THEOLOGICAL SEMINARY, NEW YORK;
AUTHOR OF 'BIBLICAL STUDY,' 'AMERICAN PRESBYTERIANISM,' ETC.

NOTE.—This Work discusses all the Messianic passages of the Old Testament in a fresh Translation, with critical notes, and aims to trace the development of the Messianic idea in the Old Testament.

'Professor Briggs' Messianic Prophecy is a most excellent book, in which I greatly rejoice.'—Prof. FRANZ DELITZSCH.

'All scholars will join in recognising its singular usefulness as a text-book. It has been much wanted.'—Rev. Canon CHEYNE.

'Prof. Briggs' new book on Messianic Prophecy is a worthy companion to his indispensable text-book on "Biblical Study." . . . He has produced the first English text-book on the subject of Messianic Prophecy which a modern teacher can use.'—*The Academy.*

In post 8vo, Third Edition, price 7s. 6d.,

BIBLICAL STUDY:
ITS PRINCIPLES, METHODS, AND HISTORY.

With Introduction by Professor A. B. BRUCE, D.D.

'We are sure that no student will regret sending for this book.'—*Academy.*

'Dr. Briggs' book is a model of masterly condensation and conciseness.'—*Freeman.*

'We have great pleasure in recommending Dr. Briggs' book to the notice of all biblical students.'—*Nonconformist.*

'Written by one who has made himself a master of the subject, and who is able to write upon it, both with the learning of the scholar and the earnestness of sincere conviction.'—*Scotsman.*

In post 8vo, Third Edition, price 7s. 6d.,

WHITHER?
A THEOLOGICAL QUESTION FOR THE TIMES.

CONTENTS:—Chap. I. Drifting. — II. Orthodoxy. — III. Changes. — IV. Shifting. — V. Excesses. — VI. Failures. — VII. Departures. — VIII. Perplexities. — IX. Barriers. — X. Thither.

'An exceedingly scholarly, able, suggestive, and timely work. . . . It is invaluable as showing, like glacier posts, the pace and direction of theological thought.'—*Nonconformist.*

'This book makes such a timely appearance, and is so entirely applicable to controversies going on at this moment amongst us, that it is sure to be read with the greatest possible interest.'—*Scotsman.*

GRIMM'S LEXICON.

'The best New Testament Greek Lexicon. . . . It is a treasury of the results of exact scholarship.'—BISHOP WESTCOTT.

In demy 4to, Third Edition, price 36s.,

A GREEK-ENGLISH LEXICON OF THE NEW TESTAMENT,

BEING

GRIMM'S 'WILKE'S CLAVIS NOVI TESTAMENTI.'

Translated, Revised, and Enlarged

BY

JOSEPH HENRY THAYER, D.D.,

BUSSEY PROFESSOR OF NEW TESTAMENT CRITICISM AND INTERPRETATION
IN THE DIVINITY SCHOOL OF HARVARD UNIVERSITY.

EXTRACT FROM PREFACE.

TOWARDS the close of the year 1862, the "Arnoldische Buchhandlung" in Leipzig published the First Part of a Greek-Latin Lexicon of the New Testament, prepared upon the basis of the "Clavis Novi Testamenti Philologica" of C. G. Wilke (second edition, 2 vols. 1851), by Professor C. L. WILIBALD GRIMM of Jena. In his Prospectus, Professor Grimm announced it as his purpose not only (in accordance with the improvements in classical lexicography embodied in the Paris edition of Stephen's Thesaurus and in the fifth edition of Passow's Dictionary edited by Rost and his coadjutors) to exhibit the historical growth of a word's significations, and accordingly in selecting his vouchers for New Testament usage to show at what time and in what class of writers a given word became current, but also duly to notice the usage of the Septuagint and of the Old Testament Apocrypha, and especially to produce a Lexicon which should correspond to the present condition of textual criticism, of exegesis, and of biblical theology. He devoted more than seven years to his task. The successive Parts of his work received, as they appeared, the outspoken commendation of scholars diverging as widely in their views as Hupfeld and Hengstenberg; and since its completion in 1868 it has been generally acknowledged to be by far the best Lexicon of the New Testament extant.'

'The best New Testament Greek Lexicon. . . . It is a treasury of the results of exact scholarship.'—BISHOP WESTCOTT.

'I regard it as a work of the greatest importance. . . . It seems to me a work showing the most patient diligence, and the most carefully arranged collection of useful and helpful references.'—THE BISHOP OF GLOUCESTER AND BRISTOL.

'The use of Professor Grimm's book for years has convinced me that it is not only unquestionably the best among existing New Testament Lexicons, but that, apart from all comparisons, it is a work of the highest intrinsic merit, and one which is admirably adapted to initiate a learner into an acquaintance with the language of the New Testament. It ought to be regarded as one of the first and most necessary requisites for the study of the New Testament, and consequently for the study of theology in general.'—Professor EMIL SCHÜRER.

Just published, in crown 8vo, price 5s.,

THE LORD'S SUPPER:

A BIBLICAL EXPOSITION OF ITS ORIGIN, NATURE, AND USE.

BY

REV. J. P. LILLEY, M.A.,

ARBROATH;

SOMETIME HAMILTON SCHOLAR AND CUNNINGHAM FELLOW OF THE
NEW COLLEGE, EDINBURGH.

CONTENTS.—Introduction.—Chapter I. The Passover.—II. The Lord's Last Passover.—III. The Passover merged in the Lord's Supper.—IV. The Ratification of the First Covenant.—V. The Lord's Supper in the Reception of the New Covenant.—VI. The Lord's Supper in the Apostolic Church.—VII. The Real Nature of the Supper.—VIII. The Specific Purposes of the Supper.—IX. The Circle for which the Supper was intended—the Qualifications expected of those who apply for Admission to it.—X. The Spirit in which the Supper is to be used.—XI. The Spirit to be maintained after Communion.—Appendix.—Index of Texts.

'*We know no better modern book more suggestive and helpful.*'—FREEMAN.

EDINBURGH:
T. & T. CLARK, 38 GEORGE STREET.

To be had from all Booksellers.

T. and T. Clark's Publications.

Just published, in crown 8vo, price 3s. 6d.,

THE CHURCH IN THE MIRROR OF HISTORY:

Studies on the Progress of Christianity.

BY

KARL SELL, D.D., Ph.D.,
DARMSTADT,
EDITOR OF 'LIFE AND LETTERS OF H.R.H. PRINCESS ALICE
OF ENGLAND AND HESSE-DARMSTADT.'

TRANSLATED BY

ELIZABETH STIRLING

AND DEDICATED BY PERMISSION

TO HER ROYAL HIGHNESS PRINCESS CHRISTIAN
OF SCHLESWIG-HOLSTEIN.

CONTENTS:—I. Primitive Christianity.—II. The Early Catholic Church.—III. The Middle Ages.—IV. The Reformation.—V. The Counter-Reformation.—VI. Christianity during the Last Century.

'Eminently thoughtful and instructive, and well worthy of being translated into English.'—*Glasgow Herald.*

'Those who cannot study the elaborate works of Gieseler, Neander, and Milman may learn from this small volume in a few hours the outlines of ecclesiastical history.'—*Manchester Examiner.*

'An interesting, able, and eloquent work.'—*Rock.*

T. and T. Clark's Publications.

Now ready. In cloth covers, 8d.; paper covers, 6d.,

(*In the Series of Bible Class Primers edited by* REV. PROFESSOR SALMOND, D.D.),

THE LIFE OF ABRAHAM.

By CHARLES ANDERSON SCOTT, B.A.,

FREE ST. JOHN'S CHURCH, EDINBURGH;
FORMERLY NADEN DIVINITY STUDENT, ST. JOHN'S COLLEGE, CAMBRIDGE.

'One of the most practical and useful of the excellent Bible Class Primers. . . . Alike in literary quality and scholarly accuracy, this little book leaves nothing to be desired.'—*British Weekly.*

'Fully up to the high standard of the best of its predecessors. . . . Even in such a brief summary as this, Mr. Scott proves himself the master of a flexible and graphic style; he takes a masculine grip of his subject, and independent thinking, as well as sound scholarship, is visible in every paragraph of the little book.'—*Christian Leader.*

'Full of practical instruction.'—*Sunday-School Magazine.*

'Remarkably comprehensive.'—*Freeman.*

'Gives in a very concisely-written and portable booklet, accurate and well-up-to-date information upon the essential points in the history of the Patriarch.' —*Theological Monthly.*

NEW WORK BY PROFESSOR DELITZSCH.

In post 8vo, price 6s.,

IRIS:

Studies in Colour and Talks about Flowers.

By Professor FRANZ DELITZSCH, D.D.

TRANSLATED BY REV. ALEXANDER CUSIN, M.A., EDINBURGH.

CONTENTS:—CHAP. I. The Blue of the Sky.—II. Black and White.— III. Purple and Scarlet.—IV. Academic Official Robes and their Colours. —V. The Talmud and Colours.—VI. Gossip about Flowers and their Perfume.—VII. A Doubtful Nosegay.—VIII. The Flower-Riddle of the Queen of Sheba.—IX. The Bible and Wine.—X. Dancing and Criticism of the Pentateuch as mutually related.—XI. Love and Beauty.—XII. Eternal Life: Eternal Youth.

EXTRACT FROM THE PREFACE.

'The subjects of the following papers are old pet children, which have grown up with me ever since I began to feel and think. . . . I have collected them here under the emblematical name of IRIS. The prismatic colours of the rainbow, the brilliant sword-lily, that wonderful part of the eye which gives to it its colour, and the messenger of heaven who beams with joy, youth, beauty, and love, are all named Iris. The varied contents of my book stand related on all sides to that wealth of ideas which are united in this name.'—FRANZ DELITZSCH.

'A series of delightful lectures. . . . The pages sparkle with a gem-like light. The thoughts on the varied subjects touched upon fascinate and interest, their mode of expression is full of beauty.'—*Scotsman.*

T. and T. Clark's Publications.

In demy 8vo, price 10s. 6d.,

THE JEWISH
AND
THE CHRISTIAN MESSIAH.

A STUDY IN THE EARLIEST HISTORY OF CHRISTIANITY.

By Professor VINCENT HENRY STANTON, M.A.,
TRINITY COLLEGE, CAMBRIDGE.

'Mr. Stanton's book answers a real want, and will be indispensable to students of the origin of Christianity. We hope that Mr. Stanton will be able to continue his labours in that most obscure and most important period, of his competency to deal with which he has given such good proof in this book.'—*Guardian.*

'We welcome this book as a valuable addition to the literature of a most important subject. . . . The book is remarkable for the clearness of its style. Mr. Stanton is never obscure from beginning to end, and we think that no reader of average attainments will be able to put the book down without having learnt much from his lucid and scholarly exposition.'—*Ecclesiastical Gazette.*

Now complete, in Five Volumes, 8vo, price 10s. 6d. each,

HISTORY OF THE JEWISH PEOPLE IN THE TIME OF OUR LORD.

By Dr. EMIL SCHÜRER,
PROFESSOR OF THEOLOGY IN THE UNIVERSITY OF KIEL.

TRANSLATED FROM THE SECOND EDITION (Revised throughout, and greatly Enlarged) of '*HISTORY OF THE NEW TESTAMENT TIMES.*'

*** Professor Schürer has prepared an exhaustive INDEX to this work, to which he attaches great value. The Translation is now ready, and is issued in a separate Volume (100 pp. 8vo). Price 2s. 6d. *nett.*

'Under Professor Schürer's guidance we are enabled to a large extent to construct a social and political framework for the Gospel History, and to set it in such a light as to see new evidences of the truthfulness of that history and of its contemporaneousness. . . . The length of our notice shows our estimate of the value of his work.'—*English Churchman.*

'Messrs. Clark have afresh earned the thanks of all students of the New Testament in England, by undertaking to present Schürer's masterly work in a form easily accessible to the English reader. . . . In every case the amount of research displayed is very great, truly German in its proportions, while the style of Professor Schürer is by no means cumbrous, after the manner of some of his countrymen. We have inadequately described a most valuable work, but we hope we have said enough to induce our readers who do not know this book to seek it out forthwith.'—*Methodist Recorder.*

www.ingramcontent.com/pod-product-compliance
Lightning Source LLC
Chambersburg PA
CBHW021803230426
43669CB00008B/616